KEY F

COMPANY LAW

SECOND EDITION

ANN RIDLEY

HODDER
EDUCATION
PART OF HACHETTE LIVRE UK

Orders: please contact Bookpoint Ltd, 130 Milton Park, Abingdon, Oxon OX14 4SB.
Telephone: (44) 01235 827720. Fax: (44) 01235 400454. Lines are open from 9.00–5.00,
Monday to Saturday, with a 24-hour message answering service.
You can also order through our website: www.hoddereducation.co.uk

British Library Cataloguing in Publication Data
A catalogue record for this title is available from The British Library.

ISBN: 978 0 340 94243 7

First published 2002
This edition 2007
Impression number   10 9 8 7 6 5 4 3 2
Year   2012 2011 2010 2009 2008

Hachette's policy is to use papers that are natural, renewable and recyclable products. They are
made from wood grown in sustainable forests. The logging and manufacturing processes
conform to the environmental regulations of the country of origin.

Typeset by Transet Limited, Coventry, England.
Printed in Great Britain for Hodder Education, part of Hachette Livre UK, 338 Euston Road,
London NW1 3BH by Cox & Wyman Ltd, Reading, Berks.

CONTENTS

PREFACE

The Key Facts series is a practical and complete revision aid that can be used by students of law courses at all levels from A Level to degree and beyond, and in professional and vocational courses. The Key Facts series is designed to give a clear view of each subject. This will be useful to students when tackling new topics and is invaluable as a revision aid. Most chapters open with an outline in diagram form of the points covered in that chapter. The points are then developed in a structured list form to make learning easier. Supporting cases are given throughout by name and, for some complex areas, facts are given to reinforce the point being made. The Key Facts series aims to accommodate the syllabus content of most qualifications in a subject area, using many visual learning aids. Company law may be a module of both law and business studies degree courses. It is also a vital subject in many professional and vocational courses. The detail and complexities of the subject can make it difficult for the student. This book aims to help students throughout their course.

The Companies Act 2006 received the Royal Assent on 8 November 2006. This is a major piece of legislation, running to some 1300 sections, and is the result of the Company Law Review which set out to modernise and simplify company law. Some sections are in force, and it is intended that most of the Act will be implemented by October 2008. It is likely therefore that the Companies Act 1985 will continue to be taught alongside the 2006 Act during this transitional period and the approach of this book is to focus on the law prior to the 2006 Act, except where the relevant parts of that Act are in force. Where appropriate, a short section setting out the main impact of the 2006 Act is included.

The law is as I believe it to be on 1st June 2007.

CHAPTER 1

INTRODUCTION:
THE COMPANIES ACT 2006

At the time of writing Company Law is in a state of transition. The Companies Act 2006, which received the Royal Assent on 8 November 2006, following a decade of consultation and numerous consultation papers and reports, will be brought into force over a period of time by order of the Secretary of State or the Treasury. Some sections, notably the provisions relating to takeovers and mergers and the City Panel on Takeovers and Mergers, are in force, but for the majority of the Act the intention is to bring it into force by October 2008.

1.1 THE COMPANY LAW REVIEW

1. The Company Law Review was launched in 1998 by the then Secretary of State for Trade and Industry Margaret Beckett.
2. It included a very large number of reports and consultation papers by the Law Commission, the Department of Trade and Industry (DTI) and the Company Law Review Steering Group. There followed two White Papers published in 2002 (*Modernising Company Law*) and 2005 (*The Company Law Reform Bill*). The latter included a draft Bill which, following further consultation and amendment, was introduced to the House of Lords in November 2005.
3. The main objectives of the Company Law Review were:
   - to provide a framework to facilitate enterprise;
   - to achieve consistency in the law;
   - to achieve transparency;
   - to achieve clarity and accessibility of the law.
4. The Review recommended that the following aspects be addressed:

- complexity of the law (overformal language, excessive detail, over-regulation and complex structure);
- obsolescent and ineffective provisions;
- relationship between company law and corporate governance.

5. The DTI identified eight key issues for the Review Panel:
   - the scope of company law;
   - the needs of small, closely-held companies – 'Think small first' was a guiding principle of the Steering Group;
   - regulatory and self-regulatory bodies;
   - international aspects of company law;
   - company formation;
   - company powers;
   - capital maintenance;
   - electronic communications and information.

6. The Act received the Royal Assent on 8 November 2006. In the course of its progress through Parliament the Bill acquired some 400 additional clauses, and the Act now runs to 700 pages with some 1300 sections.

7. A few sections are in force (see for example Chapter 12 on takeovers and the City Panel on Takeovers and Mergers) and it is intended that most will be brought into force by October 2008.

1.2 COMPANIES ACT 2006

1. The Company Law Review set out to modernise and reform company law. The extent to which this has been achieved will be revealed over time as the Act is implemented. However, some initial reactions to the Act suggest that it will fall short in a number of respects.

2. The Review aimed to facilitate enterprise by providing a framework of legislation that is clear and accessible, particularly with respect to small companies.

3. The idea of having a separate act for small closely-held companies was dropped early in the consultation and the Act,

like the Companies Act 1985, covers all companies with exceptional provisions for small private companies.

4. Corporate governance was a major theme of the Company Law Review, which can be seen in the provisions relating to meetings, shareholder engagement and directors' duties. The codification of directors' duties in Part 10 of the Act was much criticised in the course of consultation as being likely to lead to confusion rather than clarity.

5. Ironically, the use of 'plain English' throughout the Act has also been criticised for its potential to bring new uncertainty to complex areas of law which are better described in terms that have acquired particular legal meaning as a result of interpretation by the courts and long-held usage by lawyers.

6. At the time of writing, consultation is still on-going with respect to certain aspects of the Act, notably the transitional arrangements for companies registered under previous legislation and the model articles for private companies limited by shares.

7. It is to be hoped that the Act will be implemented as speedily as possible. The current published schedule indicates that it will be in force by October 2008. However, it is likely that this date will slip. Furthermore, it is possible that there will be further amendments before the Act is fully in force, leading to further confusion. It is difficult to see how the aim of clarity and accessibility will be achieved given the necessarily piecemeal way in which this major legislation is likely to be implemented.

8. The DTI's (now the Department for Business, Enterprise and Regulatory Reform) schedule for implementation (which can be found on the DBERR's website) includes some important sections due to come into force in October 2007, including:

- Part 9 (Exercise of members' rights);
- Part 10 (Company directors), other than provisions relating to directors' conflict of interest duties, directors' residential addresses, underage directors and requirement that one director should be a natural person;

- Part 11 (Derivative claims and proceedings by members);
- Part 13 (Resolutions and meetings, with some exceptions) and, related to this, ss 485-488 of Part 16 (Audit);
- Part 14 (Control of political donations, other than provisions relating to independent election candidates);
- Part 29 (Fraudulent trading);
- Part 30 (Protection of members against unfair prejudice);
- Part 32 (Company investigations: amendments).

Part 28 CA 2006 which deals with takeovers was brought into force on 6th April 2007 and Chapter 12 focuses on some of the important changes. In other chapters the law under the 1985 Act is given, with a short section which aims to provide information on key changes that will take effect on commencement of the relevant sections of the 2006 Act.

CHAPTER 2

COMPANY FORMATION

2.1 INCORPORATION

Formalities:
- Business Names
- Memorandum of Association
- Articles of Association
- supporting documents
- prescribed fee.

Certificate of Incorporation provides evidence:
- that requirements of the Act have been fulfilled
- that the company is a plc (if that is the case).

INCORPORATION

Pre-incorporation contracts:
- liability of agent who purports to make contract on behalf of company prior to incorporation
- Art 9 First Company Law Directive
- s36C CA 1985.

Duties of promoters:
Statute:
- misrepresentation in prospectus.
Common law:
- negligence
- deceit.
Fiduciary:
- good faith
- fair dealing
- disclosure.

1. A company may be created by registration of documents with the Registrar of Companies under the Companies Act 1985, registration with another public official or body (e.g. under the Charities Act 1993), by statute or by Royal Charter. We are concerned only with the first method, that is, with 'registered companies'.

2. The most significant consequence, to a lawyer, of incorporation is that a company is recognised in law as a legal person.

3. A company may be limited or unlimited. The vast majority are limited, which means that individual shareholders are not directly responsible for the debts of the company.

4. Furthermore, a number of different types of company may be registered, the most important distinction being between public companies and private companies. Under the Companies Act 1985 (CA 1985) the same rules apply, with some exceptions, to both public and private companies.

5. For many years there have been suggestions that a separate Act should be passed to cover small private companies. This has not found favour and in the course of consultation as part of the Company Law Review the idea was rejected.

6. The Companies Act 2006 (CA 2006), when in force, will, like the 1985 Act, cover all companies, with exceptional provisions for private companies.

7. The Limited Liability Partnership Act 2000 allows for incorporation by registration of a limited liability partnership (LLP). An LLP is a corporate body with a separate legal personality, which may only be formed for 'carrying on a lawful business with a view to profit'. Whereas an LLP must be for profit, a company can be registered for non-business purposes.

Public companies	Private companies
Defined by s1(3) CA 1985	No statutory definition
Limited by shares	May be limited by shares or by guarantee, or unlimited
Must have at least two members	May be formed with only one member
Minimum share capital – s11	No minimum share requirements
Designated by 'plc' or Welsh equivalent	If limited, must include 'Limited' or 'Ltd' after name
Shares may be offered to the public	Shares may not be offered to the public – note consequences of this

2.2 REGISTRATION

2.2.1 Documentation under the Companies Act 1985

1. To incorporate a company it is necessary to deliver the memorandum of association and articles of association to the Registrar of Companies for England and Wales or, for a company to be registered in Scotland, the Registrar of Companies for Scotland (s10 CA 1985).
   - Since 2001 electronic incorporation has been possible for certain users, mainly company formation agents.
   - From January 2007 an online incorporation facility is available for individual users as well.
2. The memorandum of association must contain:
   - company name;
   - country of registered office;
   - objects clause;
   - limitation of liability clause;
   - capital clause (the amount of the company's capital and its division into shares of a fixed nominal amount);
   - association clause.
3. Articles of association may be in the form of Table A, unless this is excluded or modified to suit the needs of the particular company.
4. There must be supporting documents:
   - statement of initial capital;
   - notice of intended situation of registered office;
   - statement of compliance.
5. The prescribed fee must be paid.

2.2.2 Registrar's role

1. The Registrar then issues a certificate of incorporation, which is conclusive evidence:
   - that the requirements of the Act in respect of registration and of matters precedent and incidental to it have been

complied with, and that the association is a company authorised to be registered, and is duly registered under the Act; and
- that if the certificate contains a statement that the company is a public company, it is in fact such a company.

2. The Registrar cannot refuse registration if the objects of the company are lawful, the documents are in order and the name is acceptable according to the Business Names Act 1985 (*R v Registrar of Companies, ex parte Bowen* (1914)); *R v Registrar of Companies, ex parte AG* (1980) reported (1991).

3. A refusal by the Registrar to register a company is subject to judicial review.

4. Note also that it is possible to buy a company 'off the shelf '.

5. A public company cannot start trading until a trading certificate has been issued under s117 CA 1985, whereas a private company can trade immediately on incorporation.

2.3 COMPANIES ACT 2006

Parts 1 and 2 of the Companies Act 2006 deal with definitions of different kinds of company subject to the Act and registration respectively. The main changes to the law are:

1. One person can form any kind of company, including a public company.

2. Under s8 the information required to be given in the memorandum of association is reduced to:
   - a statement that the subscribers wish to form a company; and
   - in the case of a company with a share capital, they agree to take at least one share each.

3. As a result of this the articles of association become the main constitutional document (s18). This reflects the view of the Company Law Review Steering Group that all the company's rules should be contained in a single document to avoid conflicts and overlaps.

4. There will be a transitional period for companies registered under previous Acts, whereby provisions in the memorandum

will be treated as provisions in the articles: s28 CA 2006.
5. There will be separate model articles for private companies limited by shares and public companies: s19.
6. There is no requirement for any company to include an objects clause in its constitution. See further section 5.2.3.

2.4 PROMOTERS

1. The term promoter is one of fact, not of law. A promoter has been defined as: 'One who undertakes to form a company with reference to a given project and to set it going, and who takes the necessary steps to accomplish that purpose.' (Cockburn CJ, *Twycross v Grant* (1877))
2. People who act in a purely administrative capacity (e.g. solicitors/accountants) are *not* promoters.
3. Promoters working together to set up a company are not necessarily partners (*Keith Spicer v Mansell* (1970)).

2.4.1 Duties of a promoter

1. There are no statutory duties on a promoter, except in respect of untrue statements made in a prospectus.
2. In equity a promoter owes a fiduciary duty to the company when it is incorporated. The essence of this duty is in 'good faith, fair dealing and full disclosure'.
3. Some problems arise as to how and to whom disclosure should be made. It has been suggested that disclosure must be to an independent board of directors, but this may not be possible in the case of many private companies, where the promoters may become the directors of the company. Disclosure to the members as a whole has long been recognised as effective (*Erlanger v New Sombrero Phosphate Co* (1878); *Gluckstein v Barnes* (1900)).
4. At common law a promoter may be liable in tort for loss caused by fraud or negligence.
5. Remedies of the company include:

- rescission of any contract entered into as a result of non-disclosure or misrepresentation;
- recovery of any secret profit;
- imposition of a constructive trust;
- damages for breach of fiduciary duty (*Re Leeds & Hanley Theatres* (1902). However, the scope of this remedy is somewhat uncertain);
- damages for deceit.

6. As a result of legal regulation and the Stock Exchange Listing Rules, the law relating to duties of promoters is now of little practical importance as far as public companies are concerned. It may still have some relevance to private companies.

2.5 PRE-INCORPORATION CONTRACTS

1. The company, once incorporated, is recognised by the law as a separate legal person. As such it can act only through agents (see Chapter 5). Agency problems arise when a person purports to make a contract for a company *prior* to incorporation.

2. A contract made on behalf of a company before its incorporation does not bind the company, nor can it be enforced or ratified by the company after incorporation. Early cases distinguished between contracts made 'for and on behalf of' the company (*Kelner v Baxter* (1866)), and those where the promoter signed his own name to authenticate the name of the company (*Newborne v Sensolid* (1954)).

3. The fine distinctions suggested by these and other cases made the position at common law quite complex. This has, however, been superseded by statute.

4. The First Company Law Directive art 9 provides: 'If, before a company being formed has acquired legal personality, action has been carried out in its name and the company does not assume the obligations arising from such action, the persons

who acted shall, without limit, be jointly and severally liable therefore unless otherwise agreed'.

5. This was implemented in s36C CA 1985 (the same wording is used in s51 CA 2006) which provides:

'A contract which purports to be made by or on behalf of a company at a time when the company has not been formed has effect, subject to any agreement to the contrary, as one made with the person purporting to act for the company or as agent for it, and he is personally liable on the contract accordingly'.

6. This section was interpreted in *Phonogram v Lane* (1982) in which it was held:
   - the section applies whenever a contract is made prior to incorporation, and fine distinctions as to whether the agent signs on behalf of or as the company will not be made;
   - the section applies whether the process of incorporation has been started or not (i.e. it is not necessary for the company to be in the course of being formed);
   - the section applies whether or not the company is eventually incorporated.

7. Two recent first instance decisions have further clarified the law:
   (a) In *Hellmuth, Obata & Kassabaum Inc v Geoffrey King* (unreported 2000), it was held that the word 'contract' extends to quasi-contractual obligations as well. This interpretation of s36C is consistent with the wording of the First Company Law Directive.
   (b) Section 36C makes it clear that a purported agent will be liable under a pre-incorporation contract (unless the parties have agreed otherwise) but until recently it was unclear whether an agent would be able to enforce such a contract. This issue was addressed in *Braymist Ltd v Wise Finance Ltd* (2001) and it was held that where s36C applies, a fully effective contract is deemed to have been concluded between the purported agent and the

contracting party, conferring both liability and a right of action on the purported agent. This decision is consistent with the wording of the section and with the principle of mutuality, in that a person who is liable on a contract should also have a right to enforce it.

8. Although s36C has done much to clarify the law, there is still an important defect in that companies cannot ratify pre-incorporation contracts after incorporation. It has now been established that s36C fails to implement fully the Directive (*Braymist Ltd v Wise Finance Ltd* (2001)).

9. The section has limitations:

   (a) it will not apply when a company has been bought off the shelf and is in the process of changing its name. In this situation the company does not comply with the requirement in s36C that it 'has not been formed' (*Oshkosh B'Gosh Inc v Dan Marbel Inc Ltd* (1989));

   (b) the agent must 'purport' to make the contract on behalf of a company, so the section will not apply if the parties are unaware that a company has been dissolved (*Cotronic v Dezonie* (1991)).

CHAPTER 3

CORPORATE PERSONALITY

3.1 INTRODUCTION

1. Issue of the certificate of incorporation is conclusive evidence that all the requirements of the Companies Act 1985 in relation to incorporation have been complied with (s13 CA 1985).
2. By incorporation, the company acquires separate legal personality; that is, the company is recognised as a person separate from its members, a principle established in *Salomon v Salomon & Co Ltd* (1897). It was further established in this case that the company is not the agent of its members.
3. A registered company created under foreign law is also recognised as a separate legal person in the UK (*Arab Monetary Fund v Hashim (No 3)* (1991)).

3.2 CONSEQUENCES OF INCORPORATION

1. The company is an association of its members and a person separate from its members.
2. The company can make contracts.
3. The company can sue and be sued.
4. The company can own property.
5. The company continues in existence despite changes of membership. In other words, a company enjoys 'perpetual succession'.
6. The shareholders can delegate management to directors.

3.3 THE *SALOMON* PRINCIPLE

1. The principle of separate legal personality has been described by Professor Sealy as 'the cornerstone of company law'. It is a

powerful device, allowing incorporators to manage commercial risk, but in certain situations it can be used unfairly or fraudulently.

2. The concept of separate personality also extends to groups of companies, with each subsidiary in a group having a separate identity.

3. Furthermore, as a company is not an agent of its members, it follows that, unless there is specific evidence of an agency arrangement, a subsidiary is not an agent of its parent company.

4. In the following cases, the *Salomon* principle has been affirmed by the courts.

   - *Macaura v Northern Assurance* (1925): a shareholder had no insurable interest in property owned by the company. Note that in this case the principle worked against the shareholder.

   - *Lee v Lee's Air Farming* (1961): a company can employ one of its members who will have all statutory and other rights against the company.

   - *Secretary of State for Trade and Industry v Bottrill* (1999): a sole shareholder can be employed by the company and will have rights under the Employment Rights Act 1996.

   - *Foss v Harbottle* (1843): since a company is a legal person separate from its members, a member cannot bring an action to redress a wrong done to the company – note the exceptions to the rule and see section 11.1.

3.4 LIFTING THE VEIL

1. The notion that a company is recognised as a person separate from its members is often described as the 'veil of incorporation'.

2. In certain circumstances the veil of incorporation has been lifted to reveal the reality behind the corporate entity. Furthermore, there are a number of statutory exceptions to the principle.

3. Limited liability is not a direct consequence of the corporate entity principle (it is possible to form an unlimited company), but the vast majority of companies are limited and the concept goes hand-in-hand with the notion of separate personality. If the veil is lifted this right to limited liability may be lost.

3.4.1 Judicial approaches

In certain circumstances, the *Salomon* principle can be used in ways that appear to be unjust to third parties, creditors or even the shareholders themselves and the development of the law shows how the courts have sometimes taken the view that the veil of incorporation should be lifted. Until recently the approach has not been consistent and there was no clear view as to when the courts would be prepared to lift the veil and when they would decline to do so.

	veil lifted	veil not lifted
Evasion of liability, fraud, 'façade'		
Gilford Motors v Horne	x	
Jones v Lipman	x	
National security		
Daimler v Continental Tyres	x	
Agency		
FG (Films) Ltd	x	
Firestone Tyre and Rubber Co	x	
Smith Stone & Knight v Birmingham Corp	x (but case much criticised)	
R H Rayner		x
Adams v Cape Industries		x
Single economic unit (groups of companies)		
DHN v Tower Hamlets	x	
The Albazero	x	
Woolfson v Strathclyde		x
Re Southard & Co Ltd		x
Adams v Cape Industries		x
To achieve justice		
Re A company (1985)	x	
Adams v Cape Industries		x

1. The Companies Act itself provides that the veil should be lifted in certain circumstances (see below) and the courts have also interpreted provisions in other statutes so as to require that the veil should be lifted. However, in *Dimbleby & Sons Ltd v National Union of Journalists* (1984) it was held that any parliamentary intention that the veil should be lifted must be expressed in 'clear and unambiguous language'.

2. The courts will lift the veil in cases involving national security, particularly in times of war.

3. The veil has been lifted in cases where it has been shown that the corporate form was being used as a façade in order to avoid liability or to gain an illegitimate benefit for the shareholders. Examples include:

   (a) evasion of liability to pay tax (*Commissioners of Inland Revenue v Land Securities Investment Trust Ltd*) (1969); *Littlewoods Mail Order Stores Ltd v Inland Revenue Commissioners* (1969));

   (b) evasion of a restraint of trade clause in a contract of employment (*Gilford Motor Co Ltd v Horne* (1933));

   (c) attempt to avoid an order of specific performance (*Jones v Lipman* (1962)).

4. It was held in *Salomon v Salomon* (1895) that the company is not an agent of the shareholders. However, the agency argument has been used in a number of cases involving groups of companies. Every company in a group is recognised as a separate legal person, and it has been argued that a subsidiary is in certain circumstances an agent of the holding company. If on the facts of the case there is actual evidence of an agency existing, this is consistent with the principle of separate legal personality, but the issue is usually whether an agency can be inferred.

   (a) In *FG Films Ltd* (1953) the court inferred agency in a case where a UK company was set up in order to acquire film distribution rights in the UK for an American holding company.

(b) In *Smith, Stone & Knight Ltd v Birmingham Corporation* (1939) the court laid down guidelines to establish whether an agency could be implied between a holding company and its subsidiaries. However, this case has been much criticised and has not been followed.

(c) In *JH Rayner (Mincing Lane) Ltd v Department of Trade and Industry* (1989) it was held that an agency cannot be inferred from the mere fact that the company is controlled by its shareholders.

5. The high water mark of the courts' willingness to lift veils was *DHN Food Distributors Ltd v Tower Hamlets London Borough Council* (1975), in which it was held that a group of companies was a single economic unit, thus enabling the group to claim compensation on the compulsory purchase of land even though the land from which the business was operated was owned by a subsidiary and the business was operated by the parent company.

6. This case was disapproved by the House of Lords in *Woolfson v Strathclyde Regional Council* (1978); nor was the argument accepted in subsequent cases, including *Re Southard & Co Ltd* (1979) and *Adams v Cape Industries* (1990).

7. In some cases the courts have been willing to accept that the veil can be lifted where this is necessary in order to achieve justice, for example *Creasy v Beachwood Motors Ltd* (1992). However, this view has not been accepted in recent cases, and *Creasy* was overruled by the Court of Appeal in *Ord v Belhaven Pubs Ltd* (1998).

3.4.2 Current position

1. In *Adams v Cape Industries* (1990) the Court of Appeal reviewed the arguments for lifting the veil discussed above, in particular the agency argument, the single economic unit argument and the 'façade' argument, and held that none of these applied on the facts.

2. The case signals a shift towards the view that in the absence of fraud, incorporators can rely on the principle of corporate personality.

3. This view has been affirmed in *Ord v Belhaven Pubs Ltd* (1998) and *Williams v Natural Health Foods Ltd* (1998).

4. The current situation can be summarised as follows:

(a) Although agency cannot be inferred, effect will be given to an express agency agreement between a company and its members or between companies in a group. An express agency affirms the principle of separate personality.

(b) Following *Adams v Cape Industries*, it seems that the only circumstances in which the courts are likely to lift the veil are now:

- when the court is construing a statute, contract or other document which requires the veil to be lifted;
- when the court is satisfied that the company is a 'mere façade', so that there is an abuse of the corporate form;
- when it can be established that the company is an authorised agent of its controllers or its members, corporate or human.

The meaning of 'façade'

Some guidance on the meaning of façade can be found in the cases above. In circumstances where a company may be seen as a 'sham' or an abuse of the corporate form so as to evade liability or gain an unjust benefit, the veil may be lifted. Note:

(a) The motive behind the establishment of a company may be relevant, for example if it was used as a device to conceal the true facts and to avoid limitations on a shareholder's conduct (as in *Gilford Motors v Horne)* or to avoid pre-existing liabilities.

(b) In *Ord v Belhaven Pubs Ltd* it was held that the court may not lift the veil in situations where there is no attempt to hide the true facts, no ulterior motive, no impropriety.

(c) The court was willing to lift the veil in *Trustor AB v Smallbone (No 2)* (2001) where a company was used as a device for the receipt of misappropriated funds.

3.4.3 Statutory exceptions

There are a number of statutory provisions which have the effect of lifting the veil, making directors or members liable for the debts of the company in certain circumstances. Some of the most important are listed below.

ss213, 214 Insolvency Act 1985	Fraudulent and wrongful trading
s15 Company Directors Disqualification Act 1986	Person involved in management of a company in contravention of disqualification order
s24 Companies Act 1985	Reduction of number of members of public company. This will be affected by the 2006 Act under which any company can have only one member
s349(4) Companies Act 1985	Misdescription by an officer of the company on bill of exchange, promissory note, cheque, etc
s 9, part II, Companies Act 1985	Consolidated accounts for groups of companies
s117(8) Companies Act 1985	Where a plc fails to obtain a trading certificate before trading or borrowing money

3.5 CORPORATE LIABILITY

The fact that a company is an artificial person raises questions as to the limits of corporate liability.

3.5.1 Liability in contract

Liability for contracts and other commercial transactions undertaken by companies is governed by the company's objects clause in the memorandum of association and s35 of the Companies Act 1985, and the law of agency and s35A (see section 5.4). Under the Companies Act 2006, when in force, a company will not be required to have an objects clause (see further section 5.2.3).

3.5.2 Liability in tort

1. In tort, the concept of vicarious liability allows a company to be held vicariously liable for the wrongful acts of its officers and employees as long as they were acting in the course of their employment. The employee who commits the act will also be liable as the primary tortfeasor.

2. A problem may arise in cases, such as *Williams v Natural Health Foods Ltd,* where the alleged tortfeasor is also the main shareholder and managing director of the company.

   - If s/he were held to be personally liable for the tort, this would effectively remove the protection of incorporation and, in the case of a limited company, of limited liability.

   - In *Williams* the managing director of a company provided advice which was acted upon by the claimant. The company would have been liable, but it had ceased to exist and the question arose whether the managing director could be liable for negligent misstatement, based on whether this was a personal tort of the director rather than one carried out for the business purposes of the company. It was found that the managing director had not assumed personal responsibility for the advice given and was held not liable.

3. However, it may be possible to show that the director is personally liable for a tort involving fraud or dishonesty, as in *Standard Chartered Bank v Pakistan National Shipping Corp (No 2)* (2002), where both the director and the company were sued for the tort of deceit. The House of Lords held that all the elements of the tort were proved against the director and he was personally liable. Liability in tort presents difficult issues and each case will depend on its facts.

3.5.3 Liability for crime

1. There are certain crimes which it is impossible for a company to commit since the *actus reus* could not be committed by an artificial person, for example *driving* a vehicle in an unsafe

condition (*Richmond-on-Thames BC v Pinn & Wheeler Ltd* (1989)).

2. In recent years the debate has centred on whether a company, being a legal entity without a mind of its own, is able to form the necessary *mens rea* for the offence in question. In three cases in 1944 companies were convicted of offences requiring *mens rea* (*DPP v Kent & Sussex Contracters, R v ICR Haulage Ltd, Moore v Bresler*). The principle that in certain circumstances a company can commit a crime requiring *mens rea* was recognised by the House of Lords in *Tesco Supermarkets Ltd v Nattrass* (1972).

3. Following the capsize of the *Herald of Free Enterprise*, the question of whether a company could be convicted of manslaughter was considered. In *R v P&O European Ferries (Dover) Ltd* (1990) it was held that it was possible for a company to commit manslaughter, as long as it could be established that a person who could be identified as the 'mind and will of the company' could be found guilty of the offence: this became known as the identification principle. In that case, however, the company was not guilty.

4. The first successful prosecution of a company for manslaughter was *R v Kite* (1996), in which the company was fined £50,000 on conviction. The managing director of the company was also convicted and was sentenced to three years imprisonment, reduced by the Court of Appeal to two years. In this case, unlike *P&O European Ferries,* the company was a small company, controlled by the managing director whose mental state could be attributed to the company.

5. Some of the difficulties are highlighted in *Attorney General's Reference (No 2 of 1999)* in which the trial judge directed the acquittal of Great Western Trains Ltd following a rail accident which caused the deaths of seven people. It had not been possible to prove gross negligence on the part of any individual who could be identified with the company.

3.5.4 Reform

1. In March 1996, the Law Commission published a report *Legislating the Criminal Code: Involuntary Manslaughter* (Law Com No 237), in which the Commission made a number of recommendations, including proposals for a new offence of corporate killing, separate from the offences primarily committed by individuals.

2. After further consultation and long delays, the Corporate Manslaughter and Corporate Homicide Bill was introduced in the House of Commons in July 2006 and is expected to receive the Royal Assent in July 2007.

3. The Bill abolishes the common law offence of corporate manslaughter by gross negligence (cl 20) and signals a shift from the identification principle to the concept of management failure.

4. The Bill provides that an organisation (it includes partnerships as well as corporations) will be guilty of manslaughter if the way in which its activities are managed or organised by senior management:
   - causes the death of a person or persons; and
   - amounts to a gross breach of the duty of care owed to the victim(s) (cl 1(1)).

   It is further provided that the way the company's activities are managed or organised must be a substantial element in the breach referred to above (cl 1(3)).

5. Clause 2, read with cls 3-7, defines 'relevant duty of care', which is a question of law for the judge.

6. Clause 8 sets out the factors that the jury must consider in deciding whether the death has been caused by a gross breach of duty.

CHAPTER 4
THE ARTICLES OF ASSOCIATION

Under the Companies Act 1985, every company must have a memorandum of association (s1 CA 1985) and articles of association. It may adopt Table A, with or without amendments, and if articles are not registered, then Table A will automatically apply. In practice most companies adopt Table A, but with amendments to suit their particular needs. The memorandum and articles are often described as the constitution of the company, the former dealing with the company's relations with the external world and the latter with the internal regulation of the company (see Chapter 2).

4.1 THE COMPANY LAW REVIEW AND THE ARTICLES

This is an area where the Companies Act 2006 will make significant changes when the relevant sections are in force, as described in Chapter 2 above and below at Chapter 5.

1. The articles will be the main constitutional document. Companies limited by shares will be able to adopt model articles either in whole or in part, as is the case under the 1985 Act.
2. The Company Law Review recommended that:
   - there should be separate model articles for owner-managed companies and s20(2) provides that different model articles may be prescribed for different kinds of company
   - the model articles for small private companies should be shorter than for plcs
   - they should be written in plain English, in accordance with the general recommendation of the Company Law Review that the law should be accessible
   - at the time of writing, model articles under the 2006 Act have not yet been agreed.

4.2 ALTERATION OF ARTICLES

1. A company may alter its articles by:
   - special resolution (s9 CA 1985);
   - agreement by all members (without a resolution) (*Cane v Jones* (1980)).
2. There are a number of rules which regulate a company's power to alter its articles, summarised in *Peter's American Delicacy Co Ltd v Heath* (Australian HC 1939). Note in particular:
   (a) A company's power to alter its articles may be restricted by the memorandum, since it is possible to entrench provisions in the memorandum. Any provision in the articles which conflicts with the memorandum will be invalid unless the provision in question could lawfully have been contained in the articles and the memorandum does not prohibit its alteration: *Allen v Gold Reefs of West Africa Ltd* (1900).
   (b) A company's power to alter its articles may not be restricted by a provision in the articles: *Punt v Symons & Co* (1903).
   (c) The power to alter articles must be exercised *bona fide* for the benefit of the company as a whole : *Allen v Gold Reefs of West Africa Ltd.* The 'company as a whole' is interpreted to mean the members rather than the company as an entity.
   (d) A member cannot challenge an alteration which was carried out *bona fide* for the benefit of the company as a whole, even if such alteration has affected the member's personal rights as long as the altered article was intended to apply indiscriminately to all members (*Greenhalgh v Arderne Cinemas Ltd* (1951)).
   (e) The court will generally accept the majority's *bona fide* view of what is for the benefit of the company as a whole, as long as the alteration is not one which no reasonable person could consider to be for the benefit of the company.

(f) The power to alter the articles is also subject the provisions of the Companies Act itself.

4.2.1 Statutory restrictions on power to alter articles

- s16: a member is not bound by a change which requires him/her to take more shares or in any way increase the member's liability, without the written agreement of the member.
- ss125–127: any alteration which varies class rights must follow the procedures laid down in these sections (see Chapter 7).
- ss380, 80(8): any alteration must be notified to the Registrar within 15 days of the alteration.

4.3 COMPANIES ACT 2006

1. It will be possible for a company to alter its articles by special resolution under the 2006 Act, as is the case under the 1985 Act. However, because under the 2006 Act the articles will be the principal constitutional document, the Act makes provision for entrenchment of articles (s22(1)).
2. Such entrenched provisions can only be included:
   - on formation of the company; or
   - after incorporation, by agreement of all the members of the company.
3. Provision for entrenchment does not prevent alteration of the articles by agreement of all the members or by order of the court.

4.4 CONTRACTUAL EFFECT OF MEMORANDUM AND ARTICLES OF ASSOCIATION

1. The ownership of shares in a company gives rise to certain rights and obligations. A company is an artificial person in its

own right as well as an association of its members, and is therefore able to contract with its members.

2. This is recognised and reinforced in s14 of the Companies Act, which provides that subject to provisions in the Act itself, the memorandum and articles of association operate as if they had been signed and sealed by each member.

3. Although s14 does not explicitly describe the relationship as contractual, the section is interpreted as creating a contract between the company and its members and the members *inter se*.

4. Section 14 refers to both the memorandum and articles of association, but discussion of the s14 contract tends to focus on the articles since this contains the rules for internal management of the company.

4.4.1 Special features of the s14 contract

Ordinary contract	s14 contract
Terms agreed by parties	Member usually accepts terms by purchase of shares in company
Terms provide for obligations/rights which when performed come to an end	Memorandum and articles create ongoing rights/obligations as company's constitution
Terms only altered by agreement of parties	Memorandum (objects) (s4 CA 1985) and articles (s9 CA 1985) can be altered by special resolution (75% of vote)
Rectification available	Rectification not available (*Scott v Scott* (1940))
Damages usual remedy for breach	Damages usually not appropriate (but may be claimed for liquidated sum, e.g. dividend); declaration usual remedy

4.4.2 The scope of s14

1. The scope of the s14 contract has been considered in a number of cases, which cannot easily be reconciled. The following points are clearly established:
   (a) Once registered, the memorandum and articles constitute a contract between the members and the company and between the members *inter se* (*Wood v Odessa Waterworks Co* (1889)). This contract gives rise to:
      • contractual rights between the company and its members (*Hickman v Kent & Romney Marsh Sheep-Breeders Association* (1915));
      • contractual rights for shareholders against fellow shareholders (*Rayfield v Hands* (1960)).
   (b) However, a member can only enforce those rights that s/he has in his or her capacity as a member. A claim based on s14 made by an **outsider** (that is, a person making a claim in a capacity other than that of a member) will not succeed (*Eley v Positive Government Security Life Assurance* (1876); *Beattie v E and F Beattie* (1938)). It should be noted here that 'outsider' has been very strictly defined, so that a person claiming as a director, even if s/he is also a member, will fail.

4.4.3 Cases giving guidance

1. The following rights contained in the articles may be enforced by members:
   • provision in the articles requiring directors to purchase shares from a member wishing to leave the company (*Rayfield v Hands*);
   • right to exercise his/her vote at general meeting (*Pender v Lushington* (1877));
   • payment of a dividend, duly declared (*Wood v Odessa Waterworks Co*). In this case a member was able to demand payment in cash as implied by the articles, even though the

general meeting had agreed to payment by way of
debenture;
- right to bring proceedings to restrain an act which is
outside the capacity of the company (s35(2) CA 1985) or
the powers of the directors (s35A(4) CA 1985);
- right to enforce a veto on certain acts by directors (*Salmon
v Quin & Axtens* (1909)).

2. The company may enforce a provision in the articles, for
example in *Hickman v Kent and Romney Marsh Sheepbreeders
Association* (1915) the company was able to stop an action by
a member and require that the dispute between it and its
members be referred to arbitration as provided in the articles.

4.4.4 Enforcing 'outsider rights'

1. It is well-established that no contract is created under s14
between the company and an outsider, even a director. It is
less clear whether 'outsider' rights can be enforced by a person
bringing a claim as a member, on the basis that every member
has the right to have the company's business conducted in
accordance with the articles.

2. This was suggested by K.W. Wedderburn in an important
article in 1957 and has been the subject of academic debate
since then.

3. It is suggested that if the provision in the articles relates to a
constitutional matter, for example those listed above, then a
member will be able to enforce the article as a contract, even
if this indirectly enforces outsider rights.

4. But if the matter relates to an aspect of internal organisation
or management of the company, for example the right to be
paid a salary or the right to be the company's solicitor (*Eley v
Positive Life)* then the provision will not be enforceable.

4.4.5 Recent developments

Two relatively recent developments have provided directors with alternative ways of enforcing certain rights which would be unenforceable by means of the s14 contract:

- Unfair prejudice under s459 CA 1985 – see further Chapter 11;
- in the case of small private companies shareholder agreements may be used to protect rights of shareholders and directors under the general law of contract.

4.5 DIRECTORS, THE ARTICLES AND EXTRINSIC CONTRACTS

1. Directors may or may not also be members of their companies.
2. In their capacity as directors they have no contractual relationship with the company under s14.
3. However, a company can make contracts with its directors and other third parties, which expressly or impliedly incorporate terms contained in the articles, for example articles about directors' remuneration may be incorporated in a contract of service.
4. Where an article provides for the employment of a director, but there is no contract, the court may imply an extrinsic contract (*Re New British Iron Co, ex parte Beckwith* (1898)).
5. These rights can be enforced against the company without relying on the articles, but alteration of the articles may vary the terms of the contract.
6. The articles can be altered at any time by special resolution, thus varying the terms of the contract, but terms cannot be altered retrospectively (*Swabey v Port Darwin Gold Mining Co* (1889)).
7. If provisions from the articles are incorporated into extrinsic contracts, alteration of the articles may result in breach of the extrinsic contract. A third party cannot prevent alteration of

the articles, but in such cases the company may be liable to pay damages (*Southern Foundries (1926) Ltd v Shirlaw* (1940)).

4.6 SHAREHOLDER AGREEMENTS

1. A shareholder agreement may be used in addition to the memorandum and articles. Such agreements enable the company to create an ordinary contract between the company and its members and others, including directors.
2. Such agreements will only bind the parties to it, so problems may arise on the transfer of shares as the new shareholder will not be bound.
3. The memorandum and articles of association are public documents. If these could be overridden by a separate agreement between shareholders, the principle of disclosure would be undermined. Therefore if a shareholder agreement is to have constitutional implications (that is, if it comes within the definition of s380(4)), it must be registered by the Registrar of Companies.
4. Because shareholder agreements require agreement by all members, they are generally only suitable for use by small private companies.

4.7 COMPANIES ACT 2006

1. In its report *Shareholder Remedies* (Law Com Report No 246 1997) the Law Commission considered whether s14 should be changed to state explicitly that the memorandum and articles have effect as a contract between the company and each member and between each member and every other member, but no change to current legislation was considered necessary.
2. On the other hand, the Company Law Steering Group considered that s14 'is so misleading' that it would be desirable to:

- lay down a statutory provision explaining the extent to which individual shareholders are entitled to enforce the constitution;
- abolish the contractual character of the rights.

3. In the event no substantive change was made in the Companies Act 2006. Section 33(1) replaces s14(1), with changes to the wording intended to clarify the section and modernise the language. As is the case under the 1985 Act, provisions in the constitution will bind the company and its members, and will not confer rights on outsiders. It is arguable that the section does little to clarify the law itself and it does not address the issues raised by the Company Law Review.

4. That said, the success of s459 of the 1985 Act in dealing with unfair prejudice, alongside the complexity and relative uncertainty of the effect of the statutory contract, has meant that s14 has not been widely used to enforce rights and deal with disputes that arise between the company and its members and this will probably continue under the new Act.

CHAPTER 5

TRANSACTIONS WITH
THIRD PARTIES

Does the company have the capacity to make the contract?
- Objects clause
- S35

Is the contract binding on the company?

Does the person purporting to act for the company have authority?
- S35A
- General law of agency
- Rule in Turquand's case

5.1 THE *ULTRA VIRES* DOCTRINE: HISTORICAL PERSPECTIVE

5.1.1 The contractual capacity of companies

1. Since 1856 successive Companies Acts have required that an objects clause be included in the memorandum of association and this remains the case, with some modification as to the nature of the objects clause, under the Companies Act 1985: ss1 and 2 CA 1985.
2. The objects clause sets out the activities for which the company was formed and any activity outside this statement of objects is said to be *ultra vires* the company (outside the company's capacity). At common law any such transaction was void.
3. The previous strictness of the *ultra vires* doctrine has been ameliorated, first by s9 of the European Communities Act 1972, consolidated as s35 CA 1985, and then by the Companies Act 1989, which substituted a new s35 in the 1985 Act. The rule is still relevant as an internal mechanism whereby directors may be restrained from entering into an *ultra vires* transaction. When the relevant part is in force, the Companies Act 2006 will abolish the requirement for a company to have an objects clause.
4. The reasons for the rule were:
   - that shareholders are entitled to know the purpose for which their investment was to be used;
   - it was supposed to protect creditors, who were deemed to know the contents of the memorandum.
5. The *ultra vires* rule was strengthened by the doctrine of constructive notice. Because the memorandum is a public document, anyone dealing with a company was deemed to know its contents, including its objects clause, so was deemed to know if a transaction was beyond the capacity of the company. This sometimes led to very harsh results (*Re Jon Beauforte (London) Ltd* (1953)).

6. The memorandum also commonly included a statement of the powers conferred on the company to enable it to carry out its objects. This led to confusion until the law was clarified in *Rolled Steel Products (Holdings) Ltd v British Steel Corporation* (1986).

5.1.2 Development of the law

1. In *Ashbury Railway Carriage & Iron Co Ltd v Riche* (1875) the House of Lords held that a company did not have the capacity to enter into a contract outside the objects clause and therefore such a contract could not be enforced by either party. One consequence of this was that a company could escape liability because it had acted outside its objects clause.
2. Although it was designed to protect shareholders, companies found the doctrine restrictive and ingenious draftsmen found ways around it.
3. It became commonplace for companies to include long objects clauses with a number of separate clauses followed by a clause to the effect that each and every paragraph contained a separate object of the company – known as a *Cotman v Brougham* clause, since such practice was somewhat reluctantly accepted as valid in that case.
4. Another device used by companies was the 'subjective' objects clause, considered by the court in *Bell Houses v City Wall Properties Ltd* (1966). Two main objects were followed by a clause stating that the company had capacity 'to carry on any other trade or business whatsoever which can, in the opinion of the board of directors, be advantageously carried on by the company in connection with or ancillary to any of the above businesses or the general business of the company'.
5. The law was further complicated by the distinction found by the judges between objects and powers (*Re Introductions* (1968); *Re Horsley & Weight Ltd* (1982)). In *Rolled Steel Products (Holdings) Ltd v British Steel Corporation* (1986) the Court of Appeal reviewed and clarified the law, holding that

where the directors exercise a power stated in the objects clause that is reasonably incidental to the company's substantive objects, this will be within the capacity of the company unless it amounts to a breach of fiduciary duty and the third party has knowledge of this.

5.1.3 The need for reform

1. The *ultra vires* rule has been the subject of controversy over a long period. Its application allowed companies to avoid transactions, often producing harsh results for third parties.
2. In *Cotman v Brougham* (1918) Lord Parker said, 'The narrower the objects expressed in the memorandum, the less is the subscribers' risk, but the wider such objects, the greater the security of those who transact business with the company'.
3. Furthermore, difficulty arises because the company is owned by its members, and yet it is the directors, who may not necessarily be members themselves, who conduct the company's business.
4. This leads to a tension between the need to ensure that the company's property is used for the benefit of the members, and the need not to place undue constraints on the directors' freedom to take the company forward. The objects clause and the *ultra vires* doctrine achieved the former at common law, but not the latter.

5.2 STATUTORY REFORM

5.2.1 Reform to date

1. In 1945 the Cohen Committee (Cmd 6659) recommended that a company should have the same powers as an individual as regards third parties.
2. In 1962 the Jenkins Committee (Cmnd 1749) recommended the abolition of the constructive notice rule, but did not favour full abolition of the *ultra vires* doctrine itself.

3. No change was made until 1973, when the UK's entry into the EEC made it necessary to comply with Art 9 of the First Company Law Directive. Section 9(1) of the European Communities Act 1972 (consolidated as s35 Companies Act 1985) provided:

'In favour of a person dealing with a company in good faith, any transaction decided on by the directors shall be deemed to be one which it is within the capacity of the company to enter into, and the power of the directors to bind the company shall be deemed to be free of any limitation under the memorandum or articles of association'.

This provision gave rise to considerable uncertainty and the drive for reform continued.

4. In 1986 the Prentice Report recommended that companies should have capacity to do any act whatsoever and should have the option of not stating their objects in their memorandum of association.

None of these proposals was acted upon.

5.2.2 The current law

1. The Companies Act 1989 amended s35 of the Companies Act 1985 which now provides that:
- the validity of an act done by a company shall not be called into question on the ground of lack of capacity by reason of anything in the company's memorandum (s35(1));
- *but* a member can bring proceedings to stop the doing of an act which would be beyond the company's capacity but for s35(1) *unless* the company is under a legal obligation to do the act (s35(2));
- directors have a duty to act within their powers as set out in the memorandum;
- members can ratify an *ultra vires* act by special resolution;
- a separate special resolution is required to absolve the directors from liability arising from their breach of duty (s35(3)).

2. While this section effectively abolishes the rule as far as transactions between the company and third parties are concerned, the objects clause and the *ultra vires* doctrine may still have application with respect to the internal management of the company.
3. The 1989 Act also inserted s3A which allows companies to state that their object is 'to carry on business as a general commercial company'.
4. Professor Sealy comments '[This] can be seen as a well-meaning attempt to encourage the draftsmen of company memoranda to abandon the traditional long-winded objects clause ... It appears, however, that the draftsmen have not taken the bait. Many have sought to have the best of both worlds, by continuing their use of lengthy precedents and adding a further clause listing the carrying on of business as a general commercial company as an additional object!'

5.2.3 Companies Act 2006

1. Under the 2006 Act, when the relevant sections come into force, all companies will have unlimited objects, unless a clause specifically restricting a company's objects is included in the articles: s33(1).
2. Section 33(2) and (3) provide that any change to a company's articles must be notified to the Registrar.
3. Section 39 replaces s35 of the 1985 Act, except that there is no equivalent of section 35(2) and (3). These sections were considered unnecessary because of the fact that companies will have unlimited objects, unless expressly restricted, together with the fact that s171 places a duty on directors to abide by the constitution.
4. Section 39 refers to the company's constitution rather than the memorandum.
5. It follows, too, that there is no equivalent to s3A CA 1985.

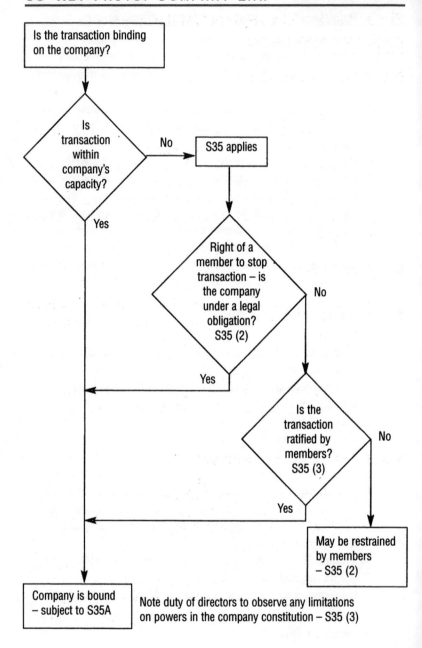

Company is bound – subject to S35A

Note duty of directors to observe any limitations on powers in the company constitution – S35 (3)

5.3 AGENCY PRINCIPLES AND COMPANY LAW

5.3.1 First principles

1. It is a general rule that, with some statutory exceptions, a person can only enforce a contract if he or she is a party to it. This is the doctrine of privity of contract.
2. The law of agency is a major common law exception to this rule and enables a person with the appropriate authority (the agent) to create a contract that binds his or her principal. Most commercial transactions are carried out through the law of agency.

5.3.2 The corporate context

1. Separate legal personality ensures that a company can contract with third parties, but being an artificial person, a company can only contract through agents.
2. In relation to transactions with third parties, it is necessary to consider both the capacity of a company (s35 CA 1985) and the authority of the directors and other agents to deal on behalf of the company (ss35A and 35B and the law of agency).

5.3.3 The board of directors

1. The directors of a company have actual authority to bind the company if they are acting for the purpose of attaining the company's objects (*Rolled Steel Products (Holdings) Ltd v British Steel Corporation*).
2. Articles of association usually provide that the company's business shall be managed by the board of directors (Table A, art 70) so all powers of management are delegated to the board. In this way the company appoints its agents and gives them authority.

3. The directors, acting as a board, are agents of the company and a third party can usually rely on the actions of the directors in accordance with the ordinary principles of the law of agency.
4. The board of directors may delegate authority to others. Such delegation, to a single director, employees or others, is common practice.
5. Furthermore, in certain instances the power of the directors may be limited by the company's constitution; for example the general meeting may have the right to veto the sale of certain assets.

5.4 STATUTORY PROVISIONS: s35A CA 1985

1. Section 35A deals with the authority of directors to bind the company and, like s35, it is intended to increase the security of third parties dealing with a company.
2. Section 35A provides that in favour of a person dealing with a company in good faith, the power of the board of directors to bind the company or authorise others to do so, shall be deemed to be free of any limitation under the company's constitution.
3. 'Dealing' covers any transaction or act to which the company is a party (s35A(2)(a)).
4. A person is not to be regarded as acting in bad faith just because he or she was aware that the transaction was beyond the authority of the directors (s35A(2)(b)).
5. A person is presumed to have acted in good faith unless the contrary is proved (s35A(2)(c)).
6. A member can bring proceedings to stop an act which is beyond the powers of the directors, but:
   - not if the act has given rise to legal obligations (s3A(4));
   - the section does not affect any liability incurred by the directors, or other person, as a result of exceeding their powers (s35A(5));

- a person dealing with a company is not bound to enquire whether the power of the board of directors is limited by the constitution (s35B).

5.4.1 Transactions involving directors

1. Section 322A modifies s35A and restricts the protection given to third parties dealing with a company in certain circumstances.
2. The transaction is voidable by the company and the person concerned is liable to account to the company for any profit and to indemnify the company for any loss arising from the contract when the parties to the transaction include:
   - a director of the company or its holding company;
   - a person connected with such a director;
   - a person connected with a company with whom such a director is associated.
3. The transaction will not be voidable in the following circumstances:
   - if restitution is no longer possible;
   - if the company is indemnified for any loss;
   - if rights that have been acquired *bona fide* for value and without notice of the directors exceeding their powers would be affected;
   - if the transaction is ratified by the company in general meeting.

SECTION 35A

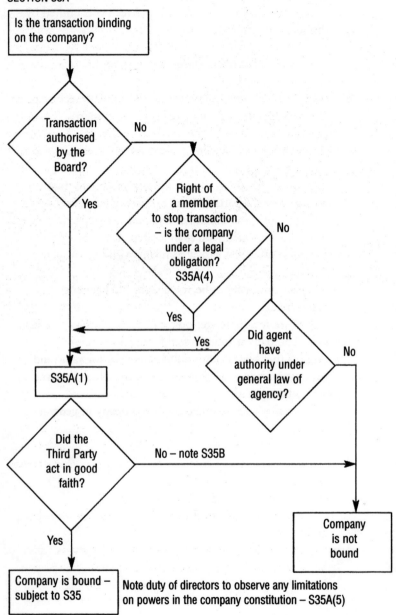

Is the transaction binding on the company?

Transaction authorised by the Board?

No

Yes

Right of a member to stop transaction – is the company under a legal obligation? S35A(4)

No

Yes

Did agent have authority under general law of agency?

Yes

No

S35A(1)

Did the Third Party act in good faith?

No – note S35B

Yes

Company is bound – subject to S35

Company is not bound

Note duty of directors to observe any limitations on powers in the company constitution – S35A(5)

5.5 OTHER AGENTS

1. Under s35A, neither the authority of the board to bind the company nor its ability to authorise others to do so can be called into question in favour of a person dealing with the company in good faith.

2. Thus the board may delegate authority to others, for example to a single director or an employee of the company. But in order to decide whether the board has in fact given authority to another person application of the general law of agency will be necessary.

3. In the law of agency, an agent will only be able to make a contract which binds the principal if the agent is acting with the **authority** of the principal.

4. Authority may be either **actual** or **ostensible** (sometimes called apparent):

   Actual authority:
   - *express:* authority expressly given to the agent by the principal;
   - *implied:* authority implied by virtue of the fact that it is necessary to enable the agent to exercise the authority expressly given (*Hely Hutchinson v Brayhead Ltd* (1967)).

   Ostensible (or apparent) authority: the authority which the agent appears to have by virtue of a representation made by the principal: *Freeman & Lockyer v Buckhurst Properties (Mangal) Ltd* (1964); *Armagas Ltd v Mundogas SA* (1986). Ostensible authority may be conferred by a particular job title, for example company secretary (*Panorama Developments v Fidelis Furnishing Fabrics* (1971)).

5. Ostensible authority depends upon:
   - representation made to the third party that the agent has authority;
   - representation made by the principal or by persons who had actual authority; an agent cannot represent himself as having authority (*Armagas v Mundogas* (1986));

- reliance by the third party on the representation (previously) that the company had capacity to enter into the contract (no longer relevant by virtue of s35).

5.6 THE INDOOR MANAGEMENT RULE

1. The application of agency rules has always caused some difficulties in company law, particularly in the context of limitations on the authority of directors imposed by the company's constitution.
2. This is because third parties dealing with a company will not usually be aware of such limitations and the doctrine of constructive notice exacerbated the problem for third parties, since anyone dealing with a company was deemed to know the contents of the memorandum and articles of association, whether or not he or she had actually seen these documents.

5.6.1 The rule in *Turquand's case*

1. The rule in *Turquand's case* (the indoor management rule) developed alongside the doctrine of constructive notice and mitigates its effect.
2. Where:
   - the directors have power to bind the company, but certain preliminaries must be gone through, and
   - there are no suspicious circumstances,

   a person dealing with a company is entitled to assume that all matters of internal procedure have been complied with (*Royal British Bank v Turquand* (1876); *Mahoney v East Holyford Mining Company* (1875); *Rolled Steel Products (Holdings) Ltd v British Steel Corporation* (1982)).

5.6.2 Is the rule in *Turquand's case* still relevant?

1. Section 35A is wider than the rule in *Turquand's case* since knowledge of a defect prevents the third party from relying on *Turquand* (*Morris v Kanssen* (1946)), while knowledge of limitations on directors' powers does not stop a third party from relying on s35A (s35B). The introduction of s35A has largely subsumed the rule in *Turquand's case*.

2. The rule may still have application where the limitation on the board's power to act is not strictly constitutional, such as when a decision to enter into a transaction is made by an inquorate board. However, some commentators have argued that the rule in *Turquand's case* is just a subset of established principles of agency and has no separate application.

5.6.3 Companies Act 2006

Section 40 CA 2006 will, when in force, replace ss35A and 35B of the 1985 Act. Section 41 replaces s322A.

5.7 ALTERATION OF THE MEMORANDUM OF ASSOCIATION

1. A company may alter its memorandum with respect to the objects clause (s4 CA 1985).

2. However, a shareholder may apply to the court for the alteration to be cancelled.

3. If an application is made, the alteration is ineffective unless confirmed by the court.

5.7.1 Companies Act 2006

1. The Companies Act 2006 requires that incorporators should submit a memorandum of association to the Registrar of Companies. However, this document will have limited constitutional significance, the articles being the principal constitutional document. The impact of the new Act on alteration of articles is summarised in section 4.3.

2. Note that under the 2006 Act a company will not be required to have an objects clause, but may limit its objects by including such a clause in the articles of association.

CHAPTER 6

THE GENERAL MEETING

6.1 INTRODUCTION

Types of meeting
Class meeting
General meeting
Annual General
meeting (AGM)
Extraordinary
General meeting
(EGM)

MEETINGS

Voting
Usually by a show of hands
with each member having
one vote.
A **poll** may be
demanded – each member
has a vote for every share
held.
A **proxy** can vote on a poll
but not on a show of hands.

Resolutions
Decision made at meetings
can be:
- ordinary resolutions
  (51% of vote)
- special resolutions
  (75% of vote and notice)
- extraordinary resolutions
  (75% of vote)
- written resolutions (s390(4))
- elective resolutions (s379A)

6.1.1 Meetings

1. A company is both an association of its members and a person in its own right.
2. Table A, art 70 provides that the company shall be managed by the board of directors, which 'exercises all the powers of the Company' (see section 8.6.1).
3. Usually, the role of shareholders in general meeting is a residual one, but note:
   - the shareholders can give directions to the board by special resolution;
   - certain statutory provisions require the authority of shareholders before action can be taken by the board;
   - shareholders in general meeting formally appoint directors and under s303 they have power to remove directors by ordinary resolution.
4. A company is an artificial person and therefore able to act only through its agents. By appointing the board of directors the shareholders in general meeting appoint agents to act for the company.
5. Further, a formal mechanism for exchanging information and making certain important decisions is needed, and, under the Companies Act 1985, the meeting is the focus of corporate decision-making by the shareholders and accountability on the part of the directors.

6.2 WHAT IS A MEETING?

1. General definitions:
   - Class meeting:
     (a) A meeting open to members of a particular class of shareholders or creditors (see Chapters 7 and 13).
   - A general meeting is open to all members and may be an Annual General Meeting (AGM) or an extraordinary general meeting (EGM).

- Annual general meeting:
  - (a) Must be held within 18 months after incorporation and then in each calendar year with not more than 15 months between meetings. If directors do not call an AGM, a member may require the Secretary of State to do so (s366).
  - (b) Private companies can elect to dispense with holding an AGM (s366A).
  - (c) The main purpose of an AGM is to consider accounts and reports of auditors and directors; to declare any dividend; to elect directors and auditors.
- Extraordinary general meeting:
  - (a) Any meeting which is not an AGM is an EGM.
  - (b) Under Table A only directors can usually call an EGM, but under s368 members who between them hold 10% of the company's voting shares may deliver a requisition demanding that directors call a meeting.
  - (c) The court may call a meeting under s371.

2. At common law, one person cannot constitute a meeting: *Sharp v Dawes* (1876); *Re London Flats Ltd* (1969).

3. But there are exceptions:
   - class meetings where there is only one member of the class;
   - private companies which have only one member;
   - under s367 CA 1985 the Secretary of State for Trade & Industry can direct that a meeting be held and fix the quorum at one (*Re Sticky Fingers Restaurant Ltd* (1992)).

4. A meeting can be held by telephone (*Re Associated Colour Laboratories Ltd* (1970)).

5. A meeting can be held in different rooms with audio-visual links between them (*Byng v London Life Association Ltd* (1990)).

6.3 VOTING

1. Generally voting at general meetings is by show of hands with each member having one vote. A poll may be demanded in accordance with the statute and the articles, in which case a

written record is kept and each member has a vote for every share held. Table A, art 54 allows a poll to be demanded by two members. Section 373(1) lays down detailed minimum requirements as to who may demand a poll at general meetings.

2. A member who cannot attend a meeting can appoint a proxy to attend and the proxy has a right to vote on a poll, but not on a show of hands. Detailed provisions with respect to proxies are to be found in Table A, arts 60ff.

4. Section 375 allows a corporate member to appoint a human representative with the same powers as an individual member.

6.4 RESOLUTIONS

1. Decisions made at meetings are expressed in resolutions.
2. There are the following types of resolution:
   - ordinary resolution – more than 50% of vote;
   - special resolution – 75% of vote; 21 days notice of intention to propose is required;
   - extraordinary resolution – 75% of vote; notice is required of the intention to propose, usually seven days for an unlimited company and 14 days for others;
   - written resolution – agreed by all members entitled to vote: s380(4);
   - elective resolutions (s379A) – apply only to private companies and are not effective unless adopted at a meeting of which at least 21 days notice of intention to propose has been given.

6.4.1 Ordinary resolutions

1. Unless otherwise stipulated in the Companies Act or in the company's constitution, company decisions can be taken by ordinary resolution.
2. Note in particular that an ordinary resolution is required to:
   - approve a market purchase by a company of its own shares (s166(1));

- remove directors (s303);
- approve compensation to directors for loss of office (s313(1)).

6.4.2 Special resolutions

1. Under the Companies Act 1985 a special resolution is required for the following purposes:
   - to change the objects of company (s4);
   - to alter the articles of association (s9(1));
   - to change a company's name (s28(1));
   - to ratify a transaction outside the objects clause (s35(3));
   - to relieve the directors of liability for any transaction outside the objects clause (s35(3));
   - to allow a private company to re-register as a public company (s43(1));
   - to allow a public company to re-register as a private company (s53(1));
   - to reduce the share capital if authorised by the articles (s135(1));
   - to approve financial assistance for the acquisition of shares in a company (s155(4),(5));
   - to approve payment of capital for redemption of purchase of a company's own shares (s173(2));
   - to approve the directors' service contracts for periods of more than five years (s319(3));
   - to approve substantial property transactions (s320(1)).
2. The Insolvency Act 1986 requires a special resolution:
   - to resolve that the company should be wound up voluntarily (s84(1));
   - in voluntary liquidation, to approve the transfer of shares to another company (s110);
   - to resolve to petition for a compulsory winding up (s122(1)(a)).
3. Note:
   - the list above is not exhaustive;

- the company's memorandum or articles may require a special resolution for certain decisions.

6.4.3 Dissentient members

1. In certain circumstances dissentient members have a right to apply to the court to have a resolution set aside:
   - alteration of the objects clause (s5);
   - alteration of a condition in memorandum which could have been in the articles (s17);
   - registration of a public company as a private company (s54);
   - alteration of class right (s127);
   - a private company providing financial assistance for purchase of its own shares (s157);
   - a private company making a payment out of capital (s176).

6.4.4 Remedies

1. Section 127: the resolution may be confirmed or cancelled.
2. Others: such relief as is just and equitable.

6.4.5 Elective resolutions

1. An elective resolution is required for a private company to elect to adopt any of the following provisions of the CA 1985:
   - variation of the duration of authority to allot shares (s80A);
   - dispensing with laying of accounts and reports before general meeting (s252);
   - dispensing with holding an AGM (s366);
   - to reduce the majority required to authorise short notice of a meeting (s369(4));
   - to dispense with the annual appointment of auditors (s386).

6.5 COMPANIES ACT 2006

The AGM has long been recognised as an unsatisfactory forum for the exchange of views and the making of decisions in modern companies, especially large public companies with both small private investors and institutional shareholders. The Company Law Review Steering Group made a number of radical proposals including the abolition of the AGM, but this did not gain wide support in the consultation.

Part 13 of the 2006 Act replaces Part 11, Chapter 4 of the 1985 Act and contains the provisions relating to meetings and resolutions. There are a number of amendments and in particular the following changes should be noted:

1. Under the 1985 Act a private company must pass a resolution if it wishes to dispense with annual general meetings.
   - The new Act reverses the situation and there is no requirement for a private company to hold annual general meetings, and it must pass a resolution if it wishes to do so.
   - Note that the duty to hold AGMs is retained for public companies, which under the new Act must be held within six months of the financial year end.
2. Decisions in private companies, which under the 1985 Act are assumed to be taken by resolution in general meeting, will under the new Act be taken by written resolution without the need for a meeting.
   - A written resolution is defined as 'a resolution of a private company that has been proposed and passed in accordance with Chapter 13, Part 2'.
   - Unanimity is no longer required for a written resolution. There are more detailed provisions with regard to written resolutions than under the 1985 Act.
3. The 2006 Act introduces changes as to how notice of meetings may be given and makes provision for notice:

- in hard copy;
- in electronic form;
- by website;
- partly by one such means and partly by another.

4. The 21 day period of notice for a special resolution is abolished.

5. On a vote by a show of hands a proxy will have one vote.

6. A quorum is one 'qualifying' person for a single member company, otherwise two.

7. There are new requirements for quoted companies to disclose results of polls at general meetings on a website.

8. There are also further provisions giving members of a quoted company the right to require the directors to obtain an independent report on any poll taken or to be taken at an AGM. These measures are designed to enhance transparency.

9. In drafting the Act the aim has been to reduce the administrative burden on private companies and to make the legislation more accessible by stating the law as clearly and simply as possible.

CAPITAL

The nature of shares:
- a share is a form of property – it does not give the shareholder an interest in the assets of the company

Rights depend on terms of issue of a particular class of shares. Shareholders generally have:
- a right to vote
- a right to dividends when declared
- a right to return of contributed capital and surplus assets on winding up.

A company may have more than one **class** of share.

Class rights can only be varied in accordance with s125CA 1985.

SHARES

Shares in a **public company** may be offered to the public.

Transfer of shares in a **private company** may be restricted by the memorandum and articles of association.

Rules on **maintenance of capital** are designed to protect creditors:
- dividends can only be paid out of profits
- shares must not be issued at a discount
- company may not purchase its own shares
- company may not give financial assistance for purchase of its own shares
- company may not own shares in holding company

BUT there are exceptions to these rules.

7.1 THE NATURE OF SHARES

1. A company can raise capital either by issuing equity securities (shares) or by borrowing.
2. Shareholders undertake to contribute an agreed amount of capital to the company and, if the company is limited by shares, this is then the limit of the shareholders' liability.
3. A share is a way of measuring each member's interest in the company. So if a company has an authorised and issued share capital of £10,000 divided into £1 shares and shareholder A owns 1000 shares, he or she will, on a poll, command 10% of the vote. The 'say' which each shareholder has is in proportion to the number of shares held.

7.1.1 Effects of shareholding

- Profits may be shared among shareholders by way of dividend;
- Each shareholder usually has the right to vote;
- If the company is wound up when not insolvent, capital may be returned to members;
- Shares are transferable and may, in the case of a plc, be offered to the public;
- Shares in a private company may be transferred in accordance with the memorandum and articles.

7.1.2 Share capital

1. *Authorised share capital* (nominal share capital): this is the total nominal value of shares that may be allotted to members in accordance with the memorandum of association. There is no correlation between the nominal value of shares and the market value. The authorised share capital can be increased by ordinary resolution (s121 CA 1985), provided the articles allow this (see for example Table A, art 32).
2. *Issued share capital*: the proportion of the authorised share capital that has actually been issued to shareholders.

3. *Paid up share capital:* the amount actually contributed to the share capital of the company, excluding any premium and excluding calls made but not yet paid. If partly paid shares are issued, the shareholder will pay part of the price when the shares are issued and will be liable to pay the remainder at some time in the future.
4. *Called up share capital:* the total amount already paid plus any share capital that must be paid on a future date as specified in the articles or terms of allotment.

7.1.3 Companies Act 2006

1. When the relevant provisions of the Companies Act 2006 come into force, the concept of authorised share capital will be abolished. Under s9 CA 2006 an application for registration of a company that is to have a share capital will simply have to contain a statement of share capital and initial holdings.
2. Section 10 provides that the statement of share capital must give details of:
   - the total number of shares to be taken by the subscribers on formation;
   - the aggregate nominal value of those shares;
   - details with respect to each class of share;
   - the amount to be paid and the amount (if any) unpaid on each share.

   Details of the subscribers will also have to be given as well as the number, nominal value and class of share taken by each subscriber and the amount paid up.
3. Under s32 of the Act a member will be able to ask the company to supply certain constitutional documents, including a current statement of capital (s31(1)(g)). This must include the total number of shares, their aggregate nominal value, information about each class of share, the amount paid on each share and any amount unpaid.

7.1.4 Types of share

1. *Ordinary shares*: Table A, art 54 provides that each member shall have one vote on a show of hands and one vote per share on a poll. The dividend is that recommended by the directors, and the amount payable on a distribution of assets on a winding up is proportional to the nominal value of the shares.
2. *Preference shares*: usually entitles the holders to a dividend of a fixed amount per share to be paid in priority to other shareholders. These may be:
   - cumulative: if the dividend is not paid in one year, then the shareholder will be entitled to receive the arrears from profits in subsequent years;
   - non-cumulative: the dividend will lapse if the company is unable to pay it in any one year.

   Preference shares may also entitle the holder to prior return of capital on a winding up where the company is solvent.
3. *Deferred shares*: these are now rare. Promoters used to take shares which would not qualify for a dividend until the ordinary shareholders had received one.
4. *Redeemable shares*: shares that are issued with a provision that they may be bought back by the company at a later date, at the option of either the company or the shareholder.
5. *Non-voting shares*: these carry similar rights to ordinary shareholders, but no right to vote.

7.2 ALLOTMENT OF SHARES

7.2.1 Issue and allotment

1. Directors may not allot shares (except in specified circumstances) unless they have authority to do so either by the articles or by ordinary resolution (ss80, 80A CA 1985). A public company cannot give such authority for a period of more than five years at any one time.

2. Shares may be issued in exchange for cash or for other forms of property, for example in a takeover the offeror company may offer its shares in return for shares in the offeree company.

3. Shares are allotted when a person acquires the unconditional right to be entered in the register of members in respect of that share (s738(1)).

4. Shares are issued when the holder's name is entered in the register of members (*Re Heaton's Steel and Iron Co, Blythe's Case* (1876); *National Westminster Bank plc v Inland Revenue Commissioners* (1995)).

5. A company may alter its share capital in accordance with s121 CA 1985 if allowed by the company's articles of association.

7.2.2 Pre-emption rights

1. Further capital can be raised by way of a rights issue.

2. A member's influence within a company depends upon the proportion of shares held. In order to ensure that this influence is not diluted, s89 provides that before any equity shares are allotted in exchange for a cash contribution, they should first be offered to existing shareholders on the same or more favourable terms. The provisions governing these pre-emption rights are extremely complex and are contained in ss89–96 CA 1985.

3. A private company may include a provision in its memorandum or articles of association that an issue of shares may be made without offering to existing members (s91 CA 1985).

7.2.3 Offering shares to the public

1. Only a plc may offer its shares to the public. Because there is a ready market for the sale of the shares, public companies are attractive to investors. Under s81 CA 1985, a private company commits an offence if it offers shares to the public.

2. The UK Listing Authority (UKLA) maintains an Official List of those securities which are deemed suitable for trading on stock exchanges and which are admitted to trading on at least one Recognised Investment Exchange (RIE). Of some 1.2 million registered companies in the UK, only about 2,000 are listed by the UK Listing Authority.

3. Under the Financial Services and Markets Act 2000, the Financial Services Authority is designated as the UK Listing Authority.

4. The London Stock Exchange operates two markets for the trading of shares: the Main Market and the Alternative Investment Market (AIM), designed for younger, growing companies.

7.2.4 The prospectus and listing particulars

1. The requirements relating to public offers of shares are now regulated by a series of EC Directives, the Public Offers of Securities Regulations 1995 and the Financial Services and Markets Act 2000, as well as the Stock Exchange Listing Rules.

2. Any company wishing to be traded on an organised market must go through a process known as listing. Under the Listing Particulars Directive (80/390 EEC) a company requiring listing must submit listing particulars, which is a public document, to the UKLA. Detailed rules in relation to this are set out in the Listing Rules with additional provisions in the Financial Services and Markets Act 2000.

3. A prospectus must be made available to investors when a company (whether listed or not) proposes to offer shares to the public for the first time: Public Offers of Securities Regulations 1995.

4. The matters to be covered in the listing particulars and the prospectus are laid down in Chapters 5 and 6 of the Listing Rules.

5. In general, the prospectus must disclose all the information which investors and their professional advisers would reasonably need in order to make an informed decision whether to invest.
6. In July 2005 the New Prospectus Directive 2003/71/EC came into force. The purpose of the Directive is to improve regulation for raising capital on an EU-wide basis.

7.2.5 Misleading statements and omissions in listing particulars and prospectus

1. Remedies are available to people induced to subscribe for shares by misleading or untrue statements under:
   - the common law, in both contract and tort;
   - Misrepresentation Act 1967;
   - s90 Financial Services and Markets Act 2000, Schedule 10;
   - Public Offers of Securities Regulations 1995, regs 13–15, if the misleading statement is in the prospectus.
2. It is a criminal offence to give false or misleading information in either the listing particulars or prospectus in connection with an application for a listing offer of shares to the public.

7.3 LOAN CAPITAL: DEBENTURES AND REGISTRATION OF CHARGES

7.3.1 Debentures

1. A company can also raise capital by borrowing, often by way of debenture.
2. There are significant differences between shares and debentures:
   - shares create rights of membership, for example the right to attend general meetings and vote; a debenture holder is a creditor of the company, whose rights are fixed by contract;
   - a shareholder is entitled to a dividend if one is declared; a debenture holder is entitled to payment of interest.

3. A debenture may be secured or unsecured. Security may be by means of a fixed or floating charge:
   - a fixed charge may be created over specified identifiable company property not dealt with by the company in its day-to-day business, for example its buildings;
   - a floating charge may be created over fluctuating assets, allowing the company to deal with the property until crystallisation (*Re Yorkshire Woolcombers Association Ltd* (1903)).
4. Whether a charge is fixed or floating is a matter of substance rather than form and neither the words used by the parties nor their intentions will necessarily be conclusive in deciding how a charge should be categorised. Cases involving book debts raised a number of issues in relation to the distinction between fixed and floating charges: see *Siebe Gorman & Co Ltd v Barclays Bank Ltd* (1979); *Re New Bullas Ltd* (1994).
5. The Privy Council case *Angew v Commissioner of Inland Revenue* (2001) went some way to clarifying the law in this area and set out a two-stage process for categorising fixed and floating charges:
   - first the court must consider the intention of the parties as to their respective rights and obligations;
   - the second stage requires the court to determine whether the charge is fixed or floating as a matter of law.
6. A charge must be registered in accordance with s395 CA 1985.
7. A floating charge crystallises when:
   - the company no longer carries on business;
   - the security is enforced by virtue of a clause in the debenture (*Re Brightlife Ltd*) (1986);
   - the company goes into administration or receivership;
   - the company goes into liquidation.

7.3.2 Registration of charges

1. Section 398 provides that a registerable charge (such charges are listed in s396) must be registered within 21 days of its creation.
2. Failure to register a charge may result in the company and its officers being fined.
3. Under s399, if a registerable charge is not registered, it will be void against an administrator or liquidator of the company (see Chapter 13).

7.4 MAINTENANCE OF CAPITAL

7.4.1 General principles

1. One way in which a company raises capital is by the issue of shares. Share capital in this context means the money raised by the issue of shares and bears little relationship with the net worth of the company as a going concern.
2. The term 'nominal capital' means the amount authorised in the memorandum of association.
3. Historically the capital contribution of shareholders was intended to provide some security for the company's creditors and the law therefore lays down strict and complex rules in relation to the reduction of capital. However, share capital often plays a relatively minor role in the financing of companies.
4. There is no minimum nominal capital requirement for a private company; a public company must have a nominal share capital of at least £50,000.
5. Capital can be spent (and lost) in the course of carrying on the company's business, but it cannot be returned to members, as this would amount to a reduction of capital, with the result, in theory, that creditors would have less security.
6. In the case of a company not in liquidation, payments to shareholders can only be made out of profits, usually by way of dividend.

7.4.2 The main rules relating to the maintenance of capital

Section CA 1985	Rule	Main exceptions
	A company may not reduce its capital (*Trevor v Whitworth*)	Court may sanction reduction of capital under s135, if authorised by articles
ss263–281	Distributions (dividends) may only be paid out of distributable profits	
s100	A company may not issue shares at a discount	
s143	A company may not purchase its own shares	Private company has power to issue redeemable shares if authorised by articles and can redeem or purchase out of capital (ss159–162). Plc can issue redeemable shares if authorised by articles, redeemable out of distributable profits or receipts from fresh offer.
ss151–158	A company may not give financial assistance for the purchase of its own shares	Can give financial assistance if principle purpose is not merely to give such assistance and company acts in good faith. Private company can give assistance out of distributable profits (s155).
s23	A company may not own shares in its holding company	

7.4.3 Reduction of capital: the general rule

1. The general rule is that a reduction of capital is illegal unless authorised by statute (*Trevor v Whitworth* (1887)).
2. Section 135 allows a company to carry out a reduction of capital if:
  ● it is authorised to do so in its articles (Table A, art 34 allows this);
  ● a special resolution is passed;
  ● the reduction is confirmed by the court.

The role of the court

1. The court's main concern in approving reductions of capital is the protection of creditors, and the legislation provides opportunities for creditors to object (ss135–137).
2. In deciding whether to confirm a resolution for the reduction of capital the court must:
  ● be assured that the interests of existing creditors are protected;
  ● ensure that the procedure by which the reduction is carried out is correct (*Scottish Insurance Corporation Ltd v Wilsons & Clyde Coal Co Ltd* (1949)).
3. The court will not sanction a scheme if it is unfair. It must consider whether the scheme is fair and equitable between shareholders of different classes and between individual shareholders of the same class.
4. If the reduction of capital involves treating members of a class differently, then unless all members of the class have consented to the reduction, the procedure under ss425–427 (see section 7.5.1) offers better protection to minorities than the procedure under ss135–141.

7.4.4 Dividends

1. Dividends may be declared as provided in the articles.
2. Members have a right to receive a dividend once it has been declared.
3. A company shall not make a distribution except out of profits available for the purpose (s263(1)).
4. A public company cannot make a distribution which would result in the amount of the net assets becoming less than the aggregate of its called-up share capital and undistributable reserves (s264).

Consequences of unlawful distribution

1. The directors who authorised an unlawful distribution are liable to repay the money to the company;
2. shareholders may be liable to repay an unlawful dividend (s277).

7.4.5 Issues at a discount

1. Shares can be issued at below their market value, but members must pay at least the full nominal (or par) value for their shares. In other words, shares may not be issued at a discount (s100 CA 1985, *Ooregum Gold Mining Co of India Ltd v Roper* (1892)).
2. If shares are paid for by a non-cash asset or assets, the rule may be difficult to enforce.
3. Section 103 applies only to public companies and requires that if shares are issued for a consideration other than cash, the consideration must be valued before allotment.
4. In the case of private companies, there is no requirement that non-cash assets should be formally valued (*Re Wragg* (1897)).

7.4.6 Purchase by a company of its own shares

1. *Trevor v Whitworth* (1887) established the principle that a company may not purchase its own shares – this would amount to a reduction of capital.
2. This proved to be somewhat inconvenient, especially for private companies, and the rule has been the subject of reform and a number of exceptions have been introduced (ss143–181 CA 1985).
3. The general rule does not apply to the five exceptions set out in s143(3), and the following three are especially important:
   - a redemption or purchase of shares in accordance with Chapter VII CA 1985;
   - the acquisition of shares in a reduction of capital duly made;
   - the purchase of shares in pursuance of an order of the court.
4. Sections 160–162 allow a company to purchase its own shares as prescribed by the Act, as long as:
   - the company is authorised to do so by its articles (Table A, art 35 gives authorisation);
   - the purchase is made out of distributable profits.
5. Private companies only may purchase their own shares out of capital, subject to safeguards for creditors (ss173–176).
6. Note: a company may not own shares in its holding company (s23 CA 1985).

7.4.7 Financial assistance for purchase of own shares

1. The general rule is that a company may not give financial assistance for the purchase of its own shares. For example it may not:
   - lend or give money to someone to buy its shares;
   - lend or give money to someone to pay back bank finance raised to buy its shares;

- guarantee or provide security for a bank loan to finance a purchase of its shares;
- buy assets from a person at an overvalue to enable that person to purchase its shares (*Belmont Finance Corporation v Williams Furniture Ltd (No 2)* (1980)).

2. It is a criminal offence for a company or its subsidiary to give financial assistance directly or indirectly for the purchase of the company's shares (s151).

3. Exceptions are set out in s153(1). Financial assistance is not prohibited if:
   - it is given in good faith and in the interests of the company;
   - the acquisition of shares is not the principal purpose, but is 'an incidental part of some larger purpose' (*Brady v Brady* (1988)).

   This section has caused great difficulty in practice and the House of Lords decision in *Brady v Brady* restricted its use.

4. In recent cases the courts have given effect to the 'commercial reality' of the situation and in a number of cases have found on that basis that financial assistance had not been given: for example, *MT Realisations Ltd v Digital Equipment Co Ltd* (2003); *Anglo Petroleum v TFB (Mortgages) Ltd* (2006).

5. Other exceptions covered by s153 include:
   - financing employees' share scheme;
   - redeeming or repurchasing its shares under a properly approved scheme;
   - paying up an issue of bonus shares;
   - where finance is provided as part of the ordinary business of finance companies.

6. The rules are further relaxed for private companies (ss155–158 CA 1985), which may give financial assistance for the purchase of their own shares if the company's net assets are not thereby reduced.

7.4.8 Remedies and sanctions

1. These are as follows:
- a prohibited loan will be void;
- the company and its officers may be fined;
- directors may be liable to the company for misfeasance and breach of trust;
- persons receiving funds who knew or ought to have known of the directors' breach of duty will be liable as constructive trustees (*Belmont Finance Corporation v Williams Furniture Ltd (No 2)*).

7.4.9 Companies Act 2006

The Companies Act 2006 will make a number of significant changes in this area of law, implementing many of the recommendations of the Company Law Review.

1. There will be no requirement for a company to state the maximum authorised share capital, although the memorandum will still have to specify the number of shares taken by each subscriber and their nominal value.
2. Section 542 provides that all shares must, as under the 1985 Act, have a fixed nominal value.
3. For public companies there is little substantive change to the provisions (ss645–651 CA 2006). However, significant changes are introduced with respect to private companies in ss642–644. A private company may make a reduction of capital by special resolution together with a declaration of solvency by the directors.
4. Under s641(1)(b) either a plc or a private company will still be able to apply to the court for an order confirming the company's special resolution to reduce share capital.

7.5 CLASS RIGHTS

7.5.1 General details

1. Different classes of share will have different rights attached to them, which may be set out in the memorandum or the articles of association. A company may alter its memorandum only as provided by the Act (s2(7)). Section 9 provides that, subject to the provisions of the Act and to conditions contained in the articles, a company may, by special resolution, alter its articles of association. A company cannot deprive itself of its statutory power to alter the articles (*Allen v Gold Reefs of West Africa Ltd* (1900)), *but*:
   - if any alteration involves the variation of class rights, then ss125 and 127 (designed to give protection to minorities in relation to their class rights) will apply and such rights can only be varied if the proper procedures are followed;
   - if class rights are entrenched in the memorandum of association, variation is more difficult and requires the written consent of all the members of the class or a scheme of arrangement under s425 (see Chapter 12).

2. Companies may issue shares such as ordinary shares or preference shares, with different rights attached to them. Class rights will only arise if the company has more than one class of share. The nature of class rights was considered in *Cumbrian Newspapers Group Ltd v Cumberland and Westmorland Herald Newspaper and Printing Co Ltd* (1986). It was held that rights and benefits may be:
   - rights annexed to particular shares such as the right to a dividend, voting rights;
   - rights conferred on individuals *not* in their capacity as members, i.e. outsider rights. These are not class rights.
   - rights conferred on individuals in their capacity as members, but not attached to shares.

The first and third categories only may be described as class rights.

7.5.2 Variation of class rights

1. The general rule is that rights of one class of shareholders should not be altered by another class.

7.5.3 Procedure for variation

1. If variation is prohibited in the memorandum, then the only way to vary class rights is by a scheme of arrangement under s425.
2. If the memorandum provides a variation procedure, this must be complied with.
3. If the memorandum does not provide for variation, rights may only be varied if *all* members of the company agree to the variation (s125(5)).
4. Sections 125–127 govern the situation where class rights are dealt with in the articles.
5. If the articles provide for a variation of rights procedure, this must be complied with (s125(4)).
6. If the articles do not provide for a procedure then s125(2) applies.
   This requires *either*:
   - the holders of three quarters of the issued shares of the class in question to consent in writing to the variation; *or*
   - an extraordinary resolution passed at a separate class meeting.
7. Section 127 gives dissenting members of a class who hold at least 15% of shares of that class the right to challenge the variation in court – but they must act within 21 days (and this may cause practical difficulties for shareholders in large companies).

7.5.4 Meaning of 'variation of rights'

The legislation does not make it clear what is meant by 'variation of class rights' but the courts have taken a restrictive view and have sought to distinguish between the rights themselves and the 'enjoyment of the rights'. It may thus be possible to make rights less effective without any technical 'variation' of rights (*White v Bristol Aeroplane Co* (1953); *Greenhalgh v Arderne Cinemas* (1946)).

7.5.5 Companies Act 2006

Changes under the new Act, when in force, will include:
1. Section 630 provides that class rights may be varied in accordance with provisions in the articles. If the articles make no provision, class rights may only be varied with the consent in writing of 75% of the nominal value of the class or by special resolution of members of the class.
2. The company's articles can provide for a different procedure, which may be either more or less demanding.
3. It will no longer be possible to give greater protection to class rights by the memorandum as a result of the much reduced importance of this document. However, rights may be protected by a more onerous requirement than that provided for in s630, which will then have to be observed. Furthermore, a company may entrench provisions in the articles (s22) and alteration of an entrenched article would need unanimous agreement of the members.

CHAPTER 8

DIRECTORS

Appointment
- first directors appointed by subscribers to memorandum
- subsequent appointment by members

May be subject to
disqualification
- Company Directors Disqualification Act 1986
- undischarged bankrupts

Termination of office
- retirement
  (i) by rotation
  (ii) statutory age limit for plcs
- resignation
- removal from office: s303

DIRECTORS

Contracts of service
- directors not automatically employees
- terms of contract must be available for inspection by members: s318.
- terms of office longer than three years need approval from members: s319

Corporate governance
- Cadbury
- Greenbury
- Hampel
- Higgs
- Combined Code

8.1 INTRODUCTION

1. A company is an artificial person and as such can only act through agents.
2. Under the 1985 Act every private company must have at least one director and a plc must have two: s282. This is maintained under the 2006 Act.

3. Section 741(1) CA 1985 provides that 'director' means any person carrying out the role of director, by whatever term described, and includes a 'shadow director'.
4. The Act does not require companies to be managed by the directors, but Table A provides for this by art 70 (see below) and most companies will have a similar provision.
5. Every company must keep a register of directors and company secretary at its registered office and must notify the Registrar of Companies of any changes within 14 days.

8.2 APPOINTMENT

Provisions relating to the appointment of directors, maximum and minimum numbers, quoracy, whether the chairman has a casting vote, and similar matters will be included in the company's articles of association.

8.2.1 Who appoints directors?

1. The first directors are appointed by a statement in the prescribed form signed by the subscribers to the memorandum. The statement must also be signed by the directors to show that they consent to the appointment.
2. Subsequent directors are appointed by members by ordinary resolution (*Woolf v East Nigel Gold Mining Co Ltd* (1905)).
3. The power to appoint directors may be limited by the articles. Table A gives power to appoint to both members (art 78) and directors (art 79) but provides that directors appointed by the board can hold office only until the next AGM.

8.2.2 Defective appointment and disqualification

1. Section 285 provides that the acts of a director are valid even if there is a defect in his or her appointment or qualification. However, s285 does not apply when there has been no appointment at all (*Morris v Kanssen* (1946)).

2. Certain persons may be disqualified from acting as directors:
- anyone who is the subject of a disqualification order under the Company Directors Disqualification Act 1986;
- it is an offence of strict liability, triable either way, for an undischarged bankrupt to act as a director without the leave of the court (*R v Brockley* (1994));
- a sole director cannot also be the company secretary.

8.3 TERMINATION OF OFFICE

8.3.1 Retirement and resignation

1. Under Table A:
- all directors must retire at the first AGM (art 73), but may seek reappointment (art 80);
- one third of directors must retire by rotation each year (art 73), but may seek reappointment (art 80).

2. Articles, including Table A art 84, usually provide for executive directors to be appointed on such terms as are considered suitable and executive directors are not usually required to retire by rotation.

3. Section 293 provides that a director of a public company is deemed to retire at the end of the AGM after he or she turns 70, unless the articles provide otherwise.

4. A director may resign by giving notice to the company which the company must accept. Table A requires such notice to be in writing.

8.3.2 Removal from office

1. Directors (either individually or as a board) may be removed by the shareholders by ordinary resolution (s303 CA 1985).

2. Conditions for removal are that:
- special notice must be given of a resolution to remove director (s379);
- a copy must be supplied to the director who is the subject of the resolution;

- the director is entitled to make representations in writing (which must be circulated to every member) and he is entitled to be heard at the meeting;
- removal under s303 shall not deprive the director of any claim for compensation or damages payable in respect of loss of office.

3. Shareholders' right to remove directors as set out in s303 applies notwithstanding any provision to the contrary in the company's constitution, but see *Bushell v Faith* (1969) where the House of Lords held that a weighted voting rights clause, which effectively prevented the removal of a director in a small private company, was valid.

4. Removal of a director under s303 may incur liability for breach of any contract of service which may exist between the company and the director (*Southern Foundries v Shirlaw* (1940); *Shindler v Northern Raincoat Co Ltd* (1960); *Read v Astoria Garage (Sreatham) Ltd* (1952)).

5. In certain circumstances, especially in small closely-held companies, s122(1)(g) Insolvency Act 1986 and s459 Companies Act 1985 have been used to protect a director from removal: see Chapter 11.

8.4 REMUNERATION

1. Directors are not entitled to remuneration unless provided for in the constitution (*Hutton v West Cork Railway Co* (1883)).

2. Provision is usually made in the articles to pay directors: Table A, art 82.

8.5 DIRECTORS AS EMPLOYEES

1. Directors are not automatically employees of their companies. A director (especially an executive director) may have a separate contract of service with the company.

2. Whether a director is an employee or not is a question of fact (*Secretary of State for Trade and Industry v Bottrill* (1999)).

3. Terms of a director's contract of service must be available for inspection by members (s318).

4. A term in a director's contract which provides that the director shall be employed for more than five years which cannot be terminated by notice by the company must be approved by the general meeting (s319).

Companies Act 2006 – summary of new provisions

CA 1985	CA 2006	Comment
282	154	Minimum number of directors unchanged
	155	New provision. Every company must have at least one director who is a natural person
	157	New provision. Minimum age of 16 for directors
292	160	Appointment of directors of plc to be voted on individually: unchanged
285	161	Defective appointment unchanged
303	168	Removal of directors unchanged
318	228–230	Service contracts: some new provisions
319	188–189	Service contract over two years must be approved by general meeting
741	250–251	Definition: no substantive change

8.6 DIVISION OF POWER BETWEEN GENERAL MEETING AND THE BOARD

8.6.1 Table A, art 70

1. Table A provides that, subject to the Act and to any provisions in the company's memorandum and articles of association, the business of the company shall be managed by the directors 'who may exercise all the powers of the company'. The article also provides that the shareholders may give directions to the directors by special resolution.

2. Where the general management of the company is vested in the directors (as in art 70), the shareholders have no power by ordinary resolution to give directions to the Board or overrule their business decisions (*Automatic Self-Cleansing Filter Syndicate Co Ltd v Cuninghame* (1906); *John Shaw & Sons (Salford) Ltd v Shaw* (1935)).

3. The right to litigate on behalf of the company is an aspect of management and as such is also vested in the board of directors (*Breckland Group Holdings v London & Suffolk Properties Ltd* (1989)).

8.6.2 Default powers of the general meeting

1. The general meeting may ratify an act of the directors which is voidable as an irregular exercise of their powers (*Bamford v Bamford* (1970)).

2. The company in general meeting may act if there is no board competent or able to exercise the powers conferred on it (*Baron v Potter* (1914)).

8.6.3 Powers granted to shareholders

Some functions and powers are specifically reserved to the general meeting by the Companies Act or the articles. Included are:

- the power to ratify breaches of duty by directors who act outside their powers (*Bamford v Bamford* (1969));
- the power to alter the articles under s9 by special resolution;
- the power to alter the objects clause under s4;
- the power to appoint directors;
- the power to remove directors under s303.

8.7 CORPORATE GOVERNANCE

1. It can be seen from the above that directors have great powers.
2. The provisions of the Companies Act reserve certain powers to shareholders, but these are often theoretical rather than real.
3. It is unrealistic to believe that in large public companies individual shareholders have any real influence on the management of the company.
4. High profile examples of corporate mismanagement (BCCI, Maxwell, Enron) reinforced the need for a framework of regulation which sets out principles of corporate governance.
5. This has been recommended by various reports:
   - In 1992 the Cadbury Committee published its *Report on the Financial Aspects of Corporate Governance.*
   - This was followed in 1995 by the Greenbury *Report on Directors' Remuneration.*
   - In 1998 the Hampel Committee published its *Final Report* and, in consultation with the Stock Exchange, produced the *Combined Code* which contains principles of good governance and a code of good practice. Companies listed on the London Stock Exchange are required to include in their annual reports a statement of how they have applied these principles and must give reasons for any failure to comply with the Code.
   - The Higgs *Report on Non-Executive Directors* was published in January 2003 and at the same time the Financial Reporting Council released new guidance for audit committees.
   - A revised version of the *Combined Code* was published in June 2006.

8.7.1 Some principles of corporate governance relating to directors

The *Combined Code* contains a number of principles of corporate governance:

1. Every listed company should be headed by an effective board which provides entrepreneurial leadership and which interacts with shareholders so that there is informed dialogue.
2. There should be a clear division of responsibilities between the Chairman and the Chief Executive.
3. The board should include a balance of executive and non-executive directors, so that no individual or group of individuals can dominate the board's decision-making.
4. Effective controls should be in place to manage risks.
5. There should be a formal and transparent procedure for the appointment of new directors to the board.
6. All directors should be required to submit themselves for re-election at least every three years.
7. Levels of remuneration should be sufficient to attract and retain the directors needed to run the company successfully, but companies should avoid paying more than necessary.
8. Companies should have a formal and transparent procedure for developing policy on executive remuneration.
9. The company's annual report should contain a statement of remuneration policy and details of the remuneration of each director.

8.7.2 Power and accountability

Directors have great powers. This chapter has dealt with some of these powers and some of the rules and principles of company law and regulation designed to ensure that directors are accountable for their actions. The following chapters continue this theme and you may find it useful to return to the diagram when you have completed your revision.

Duties & Accountability

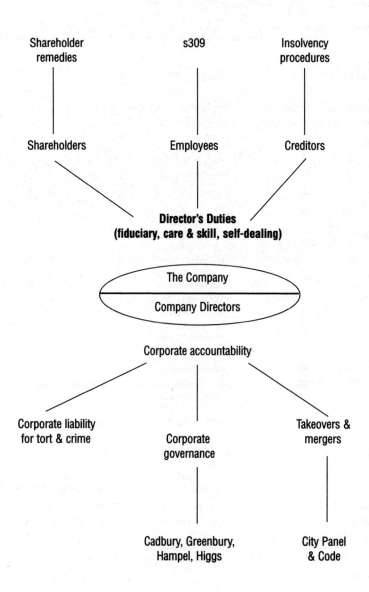

CHAPTER 9

DIRECTORS' DUTIES

Type of duty	Source	In outline...	Special points – aide memoire
Duties of care and skill	Common law – negligence	Standard of care: traditionally undemanding; subjective test *Re City Equitable Fire Insurance Co Ltd*	Note development of law: influence of s214 Insolvency Act 1986 *Re Theodore Goddard; Re d'Jan of London; Dorchester Finance v Stebbing; Re Barings plc (no.5)*
Fiduciary duties	Equity – based on fiduciary relationship between directors and company	• Duty to act *bona fide* in best interest of company • Duty to exercise powers for a proper purpose: *Hogg v Cramphorn, Howard Smith v Ampol* • Duty not to fetter discretion; *Fulham Football Club v Cabra*	Liability may not be excluded
No conflict/ no profit rules	Equity	• Personal interests must not conflict with those of company • May not make secret profit: *Cook v Deeks*; *Regal (Hastings) v Gulliver* • Use of corporate opportunity; *IDC v Cooley; Island Export Finance Ltd v Umunna*	Rules may be relaxed by provision in Articles – Art. 85 Table A. s317 Companies Act 1985 provides for disclosure to board of directors when company a party to transaction. Note relationship of Art 85 and s317
Provisions against self-dealing	Statute – Part X Companies Act 1985	• Disclosure – s317 • Substantial property transactions – s320 • Contracts for loans and guarantees – s330	Note: • exceptions to ss320 and 330 • civil penalties • criminal sanctions • overlap with no conflict/no profit rule

9.1 INTRODUCTION

1. Duties are imposed on directors by the general law and by statute. Directors owe fiduciary duties and duties of care and skill, while Part X of the Companies Act 1985 contains a complex framework of rules relating to self-dealing, disclosure and ratification. It is important to note that directors owe duties to the company, not to individual shareholders (*Percival v Wright* (1902)). As a result of this, shareholders will have no cause of action for a breach of directors' duties – only the company will be able to bring an action. Note, however, that this is subject to the derivative claim: see below at sections 11.1 and 11.2.

2. In the New Zealand case *Coleman v Myers* (1977) it was established that in certain circumstances directors may owe a duty to individual shareholders, where the individual holds the vast majority of shares.

3. In *Howard Smith Ltd v Ampol Petroleum* (1974) the general principle was established that if directors issue information to shareholders, for example in a takeover situation, they have a duty to ensure that such information is complete and accurate.

4. In general, directors do not owe duties to the company's creditors, but if a company is insolvent it has been held that they must have regard to the interest of creditors (*West Mercia Safetywear Ltd v Dodd* (1988)).

5. The Law Commission, in Consultation Paper No 153 *Company Directors: Regulating Conflicts of Interests and Formulating a Statement of Duties,* undertook a major review of the law, which it found to be over-complex and inaccessible. The Companies Act 2006 contains a statement of directors' duties in Part 10 Chapter 2: see below at paragraph 9.6.

9.2 DUTIES OF CARE AND SKILL

1. Directors owe a duty of competence to the company, but historically the standard of care expected of them has been undemanding (*Re Brazilian Rubber Plantations and Estates Ltd* (1911)). Reasons for this approach included:
   - directors were sometimes appointed more because of their social standing than because they had particular skills or qualifications;
   - the courts did not wish to deter people from becoming company directors by imposing onerous duties of care and skill.

2. This duty was categorised into three propositions by Romer J in *Re City Equitable Fire Insurance Co* (1925):
   (a) A director was expected to show a degree of care and skill as may reasonably be expected from a person of his/her knowledge and experience. *Note* that the standard of care test was expressed in *subjective* terms, so a director was only expected to act with the degree of care and skill which he or she happened to possess and was not expected to have any particular qualifications or any experience of the company's area of business.
   (b) A director is not bound to give continuous attention to the affairs of the company (*Re Cardiff Savings Bank* (1892)).
   (c) Subject to normal business practice, directors may leave routine conduct of business affairs in the hands of management.

3. In recent cases a more robust approach is discernable (*Dorchester Finance v Stebbing* (1989); *Norman v Theodore Goddard* (1991); *Re d'Jan of London Ltd* (1994) and the Australian case *AWA v Daniels* (1992)).

4. The test which has been applied in some cases has an objective element, based on s214(4) Insolvency Act 1986:
   - the general knowledge, skill and experience that may reasonably be expected of a diligent person carrying out the

same functions as are carried out by that director in relation to the company, and

- the general knowledge, skill and experience that that director has.

5. In *Barings plc (No 5)* (2000) negligence on the part of company directors was considered in the context of an application for disqualification under the Company Directors Disqualification Act 1986. It was held that:

- Directors have an obligation to acquire enough knowledge and understanding of the company's business to enable them to discharge their duties properly;
- They may, subject to any restriction in the articles, delegate certain functions to others, but this does not absolve them from a duty to exercise proper supervision;
- The extent of this duty will depend on the facts of the particular case.

6. Development of the law has been influenced by, for example:

- expectation of a more professional approach to company directorship than existed in the first half of the twentieth century;
- appointment of appropriately qualified people to designated executive directorships – e.g. finance director;
- contracts of service for executive directors which contain clauses relating to care and skill.

9.3 FIDUCIARY DUTIES

Different writers classify fiduciary duties in different ways. Some take the view that there is one fundamental duty – the duty to act in good faith for the benefit of the company and that conduct which falls into any of the categories set out below will be a breach of that duty. Others identify separate duties which have emerged in the application of the general principle that directors owe fiduciary duties to the company.

9.3.1 Good faith

1. Directors must act in good faith in what they believe to be the best interests of the company.
2. The duty is subjective: what the directors themselves consider is in the interest of the company (*Re Smith & Fawcett Ltd* (1942)).
3. This is another example of the reluctance of judges to become involved in consideration of commercial decisions taken by company directors. 'The best interests of the company' does not only mean the company as a separate entity, but includes the interests of shareholders as a body.
4. In addition, s309 CA 1985 provides that directors must have regard to 'the interests of the Company's employees in general as well as the interests of members'. This does not, however, create any right of action by employees.

9.3.2 Exercise of powers

1. Directors must not exercise the powers conferred on them for purposes different from those for which they were conferred.
2. Transactions entered into by the company's directors must be *intra vires*. This is now covered by s35 CA 1985 (see Chapter 5).
3. If powers are given to directors for a particular purpose they must not be used for some other purpose and directors must not use their powers to further their own personal interests (*Lee Panavision Ltd v Lee Lighting Ltd* (1992)).
4. A number of cases involve the allotment of shares. It is a breach of duty to allot shares to avoid a takeover (*Hogg v Cramphorn Ltd* (1967)) or to alter the weight of shareholder votes to influence the outcome of a takeover bid (*Howard Smith Ltd v Ampol Ltd* (1974)).
5. But note that acts in breach of the proper purpose rule can be ratified (*Bamford v Bamford* (1970)).

9.3.3 No fetter on discretion

1. Directors must not fetter their discretion as to how they shall act, but note that it is not a breach of duty for directors to enter into a binding contract which may have the effect of fettering their discretion at a later date, if they believe the agreement to be in the best interests of the company (*Fulham Football Club v Cabra Estates plc* (1994); *Dawsons International plc v Coats Patons plc* (1989)).

9.4 CONFLICTS OF INTEREST AND SECRET PROFITS

Company directors have enormous powers within their companies, and potentially have wide opportunity to abuse their position. Self-dealing is regulated by the no-conflict and no-profit rules as well as under Part X of the Companies Act 1985.

9.4.1 The no-conflict rule

1. The general principle was stated in *Aberdeen Railway Company v Blaikie Bros* (1854): 'it is a rule of universal application that no one, having such (fiduciary) duties to discharge, shall be allowed to enter into engagements in which he has, or can have, a personal interest conflicting, or which possibly may conflict, with the interests of those whom he is bound to protect'.

2. A director must not compete with his or her company (*Hivac v Park Royal* (1946)).

3. The consequences of conflict of interest are:
- the contract is voidable;
- the director must account for any gains.

4. But note that a director may enter into a transaction in which he has a conflict of interest if s/he has the informed consent of shareholders in general meeting.

5. Statutory disclosure – s317 CA 1985 imposes a duty to disclose any interest in a contract or a proposed contract with the company to the board of directors. Failure to disclose under s317 does not affect the validity of the contract, but the director concerned may be fined.
6. This applies even in the case of a company with a sole director (*Neptune (Vehicle Washing Equipment) Ltd v Fitzgerald* (1995)).
7. Disclosure must be to an independent board and the function of receiving disclosures cannot be delegated to a committee of the board (*Guinness plc v Saunders* (1990)).
8. A company's articles of association may allow directors to enter into such transactions where the interest is disclosed – see Table A, art 85.
9. If the company's articles include a requirement to disclose, failure to do so will be a breach of duty under the articles and will make the contract voidable.

9.4.2 The no-profit rule

1. A person who is in a fiduciary position must not, without disclosure, make a profit from that position (*Cook v Deeks* (1916); *Regal (Hastings) v Gulliver* (1942)).
2. The rule is strict and it is sufficient that the director makes a profit: there is no need for the company to make a corresponding loss.
3. The use of a corporate opportunity is a particular example of profit-making by directors. A corporate opportunity is regarded as a corporate asset, which directors may not use for their own benefit.
4. This applies even if it would be impossible for the company itself to make use of the opportunity (*Industrial Development Consultants Ltd v Cooley* (1972).
5. In some recent cases factors such as the nature of the corporate opportunity and the timing of taking it up have been taken into account, for example *Island Export Finance*

Ltd v Umunna (1986) where the court found for the director. However, none of these cases is inconsistent with the general rule, and in other examples (*CMS Dolphin Ltd v Simonet* (2001) and *Bhullar v Bhullar* (2003)) it was held that the directors had acted in breach of their fiduciary duties. In the latter case Jonathan Parker LJ held that the no-profit and no-conflict rules are universal and inflexible.

9.4.3 Liability

1. A director in breach of the no-profit rule is liable as a constructive trustee, giving the company a proprietary right in any benefit gained.
2. Any attempt to exempt a director from liability for breach of duty by a provision in the articles or other document is void (s310 CA 1985).
3. By virtue of s310(3) a company can insure its directors against liability for breach of duty, but not for any criminal liability.
4. In an action involving breach of duty, a court may relieve a director of liability, in whole or in part, if the director has acted honestly and it appears to the court that s/he should be excused in the light of all the circumstances (s727 CA 1985), see for example *Re Duomatic Ltd* (1969).

9.5 SELF-DEALING – STATUTORY PROVISIONS

There are a number of statutory provisions in Part X which reinforce and sometimes appear to overlap with directors' fiduciary duties.

Section	Summary	Penalty
s317	Directors must disclose any interest in a contract with the company at a meeting of the board of directors	Fine (s317(7))
s318	Directors' service contracts are open to inspection	Fine (s318(8))
s319	Director's contract for more than five years must be approved by resolution of general meeting	Any term contravening s319 is void
s320	Substantial property transactions: directors shall not acquire substantial non-cash assets from the company and the company shall not acquire such assets from directors unless approved by the general meeting (note exceptions– s321)	Transaction is voidable at option of company – directors liable to account or to indemnify company (s322(3))

9.5.1 Loans to directors: ss330–341

1. A company may not make a loan to one of its directors or a director of its holding company: s330.
2. A company may not give a guarantee or provide collateral security for a loan made by someone else to one of its directors or to a director of its holding company.
3. Any transaction which contravenes s330 (to which there are exceptions) is voidable by the company unless a third party has acquired rights *bona fide* for value without notice.

9.6 REFORM

1. The law on directors' duties is a complex web of common law, fiduciary and statutory rules and principles, some of which overlap and which are sometimes not entirely consistent with one another.

2. The reform of the law has been the subject of extensive review and consultation by the Law Commission and the Company Law Review.

3. The following issues, associated with the reform of company law as a whole, were considered by the Law Commission in their Consultation Paper no. 153 *Regulating Conflicts of Interest:*
- efficiency
- overregulation
- self-regulation
- legislation drafting
- codification
- decriminalisation
- EC harmonisation.

4. A number of proposals for reform were made and the Commission sought views on the following options:
- comprehensive codification of the law of directors' duties;
- partial codification of the law;
- a statutory statement of guidance, which would not replace the general law;
- a non-binding statement of the major duties to be inserted into various official documents, e.g. annual accounts;
- authoritative pamphlets summarising the duties of directors.

5. Following consultation, in *Company Directors: Regulating Conflicts of Interest and Formulating a Statement of Duties* (Law Com No 261 1999), the Law Commission recommended:
- codification of the main duties of company directors;
- that the statutory provisions should be printed on the form signed by directors on appointment.

9.6.1 Companies Act 2006

1. The duties of directors are set out in Part 10, Chapter 2 of the new Act. This is based on the Company Law Review recommendation that there should be a statement of directors' duties in order to:
   - achieve clarity and accessibility of the law;
   - make development of the law in this area more predictable;
   - correct perceived defects in the law relating to conflicts of interest.

   It is arguable that the aims of the Company Law Review have not been achieved by Chapter 2. The use of plain English, rather than the well-recognised terms of the common law, are likely to cause confusion rather than clarify the law, and it is likely that the provisions will be the subject of extensive interpretation by the courts.

2. The Act provides:
   - s170(1) – Duties are owed to the company and can only be enforced by the company. Note however that the Act provides for derivative claims – see Chapter 11 below.
   - s170(3) provides that the statement of duties replaces the rules and principles of the common law and equity with respect to directors' duties.
   - s170(4) provides that the duties will be applied and interpreted in the same way as the common law and equitable principles.
   - s171 deals with a duty to act within powers, including a requirement to act in accordance with the company's constitution and for directors to exercise their powers for the purpose for which they were given.
   - s172 sets out the duty to promote the success of the company for the benefit of its members as a whole. Section 172(1) lists a number of factors to be taken into account, including the interests of the company's employees, the need to foster business relationships with suppliers, customers and others and the impact of the company's

operations on the community and the environment, the desirability of the company maintaining a reputation for high standards of business conduct and the need to act fairly as between members of the company. This duty to promote the success of the company has effect subject to the requirement, in certain circumstances, for directors to consider the interests of the company's creditors.

- s173 provides that directors have a duty to exercise independent judgment and not to fetter their discretion.
- s174 sets out the duty to exercise reasonable care, skill and diligence. The test to be applied is the same as that in s214 Insolvency Act 1986, reflecting the recommendations of the Company Law Review and recent case law.
- s175 – duty to avoid conflicts of interest. This section makes changes to the current law as to how a conflict may be authorised. The directors of a company may authorise a conflict in a quorate meeting of independent directors in accordance with s 175(5) and (6). These subsections provide that authorisation will be valid as long as in a private company there is no provision in the constitution that prohibits authorisation by the board and in a public company there is an express provision in the constitution permitting authorisation.
- s176 – duty not to accept benefits from third parties. There are no provisions as to authorisation equivalent to those in s175 and it seems that the acceptance of benefits can only be authorised by the members.
- s177 – duty to declare an interest in a proposed transaction with the company to the other directors.
- Both s175 and s177 should be read with s180, which deals with issues involving authorisation by either directors or members.

CHAPTER 10

INSIDER DEALING
AND MARKET ABUSE

Can be committed by:
- dealing in price affected securities
- encouraging another to do so
- disclosing information

Insider is one who:
- obtains information (being a director, employee or shareholder)
- has access to information through position
- has inside information from one of the above

INSIDER DEALING
Part V Criminal Justice Act 1993

A person has information as an insider if:
- the information is, and he knows that it is, inside information, and
- s/he has the information and knows that s/he has it, from an inside source

Dealing is:
- acquiring or disposing of securities; or
- procuring an acquisition or disposal

Inside information
- relates to particular securities
- is specific or precise
- has not been made public
- is likely to have significant effect on price

10.1 INTRODUCTION

1. Insider dealing has been defined by Farrar as 'The use by an insider of price-sensitive information (known to him but not generally and which he has acquired by virtue of his position) to trade to his advantage in the securities of a company'.

2. In recent years such conduct has been seen as a breach of trust by a person in a fiduciary position and as a fraud on other investors. Since 1980, it has been a criminal offence. The law was revised in the Company Securities (Insider Dealing) Act 1985 and amended by the Financial Services Act 1986.

3. In 1989, an EC Directive (89/592/EEC) was adopted. This was designed to ensure that regulation of insider dealing was coordinated across member states and required that certain changes be made to the UK law. The new law, now more focused on control of securities markets than on abuse of confidential information, is contained in the Criminal Justice Act 1993.

4. Some commentators argue against the criminalisation of insider dealing. Professor H.G. Manne in particular has put up a defence of the practice on the grounds that:
   - insider dealing should be seen as a legitimate benefit of management and a reward for entrepreneurial ability;
   - it is a 'victimless crime' since the fact that one party may have had inside information was irrelevant to the other party's decision to buy or sell;
   - it brings information to the market quickly;
   - it is notoriously difficult to prove and enforce and it is therefore futile to have the offence on the statute book.

5. However, these arguments have not been widely accepted and it is argued on the other hand that:
   - it involves an improper use of confidential information;
   - it is contrary to the basic notion of market fairness as it places the insider at an unfair advantage.
   This view has prevailed in Europe.

10.2 THE OFFENCE

1. The offence itself is set out in s52 CJA 1993, and the terms used in s52 are defined in ss54–60. S53 provides for a range of defences.
2. Under s52 an individual, who has information as an insider, may commit the offence in three ways:
   - s52(1) dealing in price affected securities as principal or agent;
   - s52(2)(a) encouraging another to do so;
   - s52(2)(b) disclosing information otherwise than in the proper performance of his functions.
3. The offence extends only to regulated markets, or in circumstances where the person dealing relies on a professional intermediary or is himself a professional intermediary.

10.2.1 Securities

Section 54 defines securities widely, to include certain options and futures as well as shares and debt securities.

10.2.2 Dealing

Section 55(1) provides that a person deals if he:
- acquires or disposes of the securities (whether as principal or agent) *or*
- procures, directly or indirectly, an acquisition or disposal of the securities by any other person.

10.2.3 Inside information

Under s56, inside information:
- relates to particular securities or to a particular issue of securities… not to securities generally;
- is specific or precise;

- has not been made public;
- would be likely to have a significant effect on the price of the securities if it were made public.

10.2.4 Price affected securities

These are securities whose price is likely to be significantly affected if an item of inside information were made public.

10.2.5 Who can commit the offence?

1. Under s57 the offence can be committed only by a person who has information as an insider, i.e.:
   - has information (which is, and which s/he knows is, inside information) as an insider, *or*
   - has the information, and knows that he has it from an inside source.
2. An **insider** is defined as:
   - an individual who obtains information through being a director, employee or shareholder of the issuer of securities, *or*
   - an individual who has access to information by virtue of his employment, office or profession, whether or not his employment is with the issuer of securities, *or*
   - those who have inside information 'the direct or indirect source of which is a person falling into either of the first two categories'.
3. The wording of this section is different from that in the Company Securities (Insider Dealing) Act 1985, which required, in the case of a tippee, that the information had been 'knowingly obtained'. The difficulties discussed in *Attorney General's Reference No 1 of 1988* (1989) have been overcome by the rewording.
4. There is an exemption for market makers in relation to dealing or encouraging others to deal by s53(4), as long as they act in good faith and in the normal course of business.

10.2.6 When is information made public?

1. Under s58(1) information is made public if:
   - it is published in accordance with the rules of a regulated market for the purpose of informing investors and their professional advisers;
   - it is contained in records which are open to inspection by the public;
   - it can be readily acquired by those likely to deal in any securities to which the information relates, or of an issuer to which the information relates;
   - it is derived from information which has been made public.
2. S58(3) is also relevant and provides that information may be treated as made public even though:
   - it can only be acquired by persons exercising diligence or expertise;
   - it is communicated to a section of the public and not to the public at large;
   - it can be acquired only by observation;
   - it is communicated only on payment of a fee;
   - it is published only outside the United Kingdom.

10.2.7 Defences

1. Section 53 provides the following defences in relation to both dealing and encouraging:
   - that the defendant did not expect the dealing to result in a profit (or avoid a loss) attributable to the fact that the information was price sensitive;
   - that s/he reasonably believed that the information had been disclosed;
   - that s/he would have done what s/he did even if s/he had not had the information.
2. In relation to disclosing the defences are:
   - that s/he did not expect any person to deal in the securities because of the disclosure;

- that s/he did not expect the dealing to result in a profit attributable to the fact that the information was price sensitive.

10.2.8 Penalties

1. The offence is triable either way.
2. Maximum penalty on conviction on indictment is seven years imprisonment and/or a fine on which there is no limit, s61(1). *R v Collier* (1987, unreported) is one of the few convictions leading to imprisonment.
3. Any transaction entered into in contravention of the act will stand, s63, but at common law it may be unenforceable (*Chase Manhatten v Goodman* (1990)).

10.2.9 Procedure

A prosecution can be instituted only by or with the consent of the Secretary of State for Trade and Industry or the DPP. Suspected cases may be referred to the DTI from the Stock Exchange, which monitors the market.

10.3 UK LISTING AUTHORITY MODEL CODE

1. Listed companies in the UK must have internal rules to govern dealings in securities by its directors, which must be at least as rigorous as the UKLA Model Code.
2. The Code lays down a number of principles to be followed by directors when dealing in their companies' securities, including the following:
   - A director of a listed company must notify the chairman (or another designated director) in advance of dealing in the company's securities. Dealings by the chairman or designated director must be notified to the board. A record of notifications and clearances must be kept.

- A director of a listed company must not buy the company's securities during a 'close period', that is the two months before the preliminary announcements of its half-yearly and annual results or the month before the announcement of its quarterly results.

10.4 MARKET ABUSE

1. It has been argued that insider dealing should give rise to civil liability as well as criminal prosecution.
2. The Financial Services and Markets Act 2000 creates a statutory framework for the control of certain kinds of behaviour deemed to be unacceptable to the market, but falling short of criminal liability. The Act makes provision for civil liability in cases involving market abuse.

10.4.1 What is market abuse?

Market abuse is defined in s118 FSMA 2000. Initially three types of behaviour were governed by the Act, but following the implementation of the Market Abuse Directive (2003/6/EC) there are now seven. Examples of behaviour that amounts to market abuse include:
- misuse of information not generally available;
- giving a false or misleading impression of the price or value of investments;
- behaviour that may distort the market;
- improper disclosure of inside information to another person by an insider.

10.4.2 Enforcement

1. Enforcement of the market abuse provisions is the responsibility of the Financial Services Authority (FSA).
2. A range of sanctions is available to the FSA, from prosecuting through the courts for insider dealing to imposing its own sanctions, including a fine or a public reprimand.

CHAPTER 11

SHAREHOLDER REMEDIES

Common law remedies

Exceptions to the rule in *Foss v Harbottle*
- *ultra vires* or illegal transactions (but see s35 CA 1985)
- personal rights infringed
- special majority needed but not obtained
- Fraud on the minority – derivative action

SHAREHOLDER REMEDIES

Unfair prejudice
Ss459–461 CA 1985
Meaning of unfair prejudice
- must be unfair and prejudicial
- 'reasonable bystander'
- no requirement of intention or bad faith
- may include failure to meet 'legitimate expectations' of shareholder

Just and equitable winding up
S122(1)(g) IA 1986
Reasons for use of remedy
- deadlock
- lack of probity
- loss of substratum
- breakdown of trust in quasi-partnership

Statutory remedies

11.1 THE RULE IN *FOSS V HARBOTTLE*

1. Responsibility for decision-making in a company lies with either the board of directors or the shareholders in general meeting, by consent of the majority.
2. It is important to note that directors owe their duties to the company and as the company is recognised as a separate legal person, if a wrong is done to the company, the proper person to sue the wrongdoer is the company itself: this is the rule in *Foss v Harbottle* (1843).
3. There are said to be two elements to the rule:
   - the proper claimant in an action in respect of a wrong alleged to be done to a company is the company itself;
   - the principle of majority rule: where the alleged wrong is a transaction which could be made binding on the company by a simple majority of the members, no individual member can bring an action in respect of that transaction (*Edwards v Halliwell* (1950)). In other words, the courts will not interfere in the internal management of a company.
4. This can lead to difficulty if the directors are the wrongdoers since it would normally be the board of directors that would instigate legal action on behalf of the company (Table A, art 70, *Breckland Group Holdings Ltd v London & Suffolk Property Holdings Ltd* (1989)). To resolve this difficulty the courts may exceptionally allow an individual shareholder to bring an action on behalf of the company.

11.2 SHAREHOLDER REMEDIES: THE COMMON LAW

11.2.1 Personal and derivative claims

1. An individual shareholder may initiate litigation to enforce **personal** rights.

2. However, the right to litigate on behalf of the company is generally reserved to the board of directors: *Breckland Group Holdings Ltd v London & Suffolk Properties Ltd* (1998).

3. A **derivative** claim is one where the right of action is derived from the company and is exercised on behalf of the company.

4. A derivative claim arises only when proceedings cannot be taken in the name of the company itself, because:
   - the directors have decided not to sue;
   - the members have decided not to sue, in circumstances where they have the power to initiate litigation;
   - the shareholders have ratified the act in question.

11.2.2 Exceptions to the rule in *Foss v Harbottle*

1. Where the transaction is *ultra vires* or illegal, this may give rise to a personal action to restrain the company from carrying it out. In the case of *ultra vires* transactions, the exception has been circumscribed by s35 CA 1985.

2. Where the transaction requires a special majority but agreement has, for example, been achieved by an ordinary resolution: *Edwards v Halliwell* (1950).

3. Where personal rights of a shareholder are infringed, for example:
   (a) dividends paid in the form of bonds when the articles required payment in cash (*Wood v Odessa Waterworks Co* (1889));
   (b) a member's vote improperly rejected by the chairman of a general meeting (*Pender v Lushington* (1877));
   (c) failure by directors to allow a veto of a decision as provided in the articles (*Quin & Axtens Ltd v Salmon* (1909)).

   In the context of the above examples, note the relevance of the statutory contract (s14 CA 1985).

4. In all the above cases, a member has a personal right to bring legal proceedings in the ordinary way.

5. The true exception to the rule in *Foss v Harbottle*, where the claim derives from the company and is brought by a member on behalf of the company, is where the transaction amounts to a fraud on the minority. Such action will be taken by means of the procedure known as the derivative claim. The shareholder must establish:
   - 'fraud on the minority', and
   - that the wrongdoers are in control of the company.

What is fraud in this context?

1. This includes fraud in the wide sense of a misuse of power, for example:
   - directors using company property to benefit themselves (*Alexander v Automatic Telephone Co* (1900));
   - directors diverting company business for their own advantage (*Cook v Deeks* (1916));
   - using voting power not for the benefit of the company but for the benefit of the majority and to the disadvantage of the minority (*Estmanco (Kilner House) Ltd v Greater London Council* (1982)).
2. Negligence on its own does not amount to fraud (*Pavlides v Jensen* (1956)).
3. But 'self-seeking' negligence where the defendant has benefited from the transaction is within the meaning of fraud (*Daniels v Daniels* (1978)). Such breaches of duty are not ratifiable, so the principle of majority rule will not apply.

Wrongdoer control

It must be established that the company is not able to institute proceedings in its own name.

11.2.3 Restrictions on derivative claims

1. The courts have been reluctant to allow the widespread use of derivative claims for the following reasons:
   - The derivative claim undermines the concept of majority rule;
   - judicial reluctance to become involved in disputes over management and business policy;
   - the floodgates argument;
   - difficulties of proof, leading to protracted litigation;
   - cost and the question of who should pay. The company will benefit if the action succeeds, but does not want to undertake litigation (*Wallersteiner v Moir (No 2)* (1975)).

   In appropriate circumstances the courts will make a Wallersteiner order, ordering the company to fund the litigation.

2. A restrictive view of the scope of the derivative claim has been taken, for example in *Prudential Assurance Ltd v Newman Industries* (1981) where it was held that there should be a preliminary action to establish that a there was a *prima facie* case, thereby extending the proceedings. Furthermore, claims have not been allowed to proceed in certain circumstances, for example:
   - where the court took the view that a majority within the minority of shareholders who were independent of the wrongdoers did not want to proceed with the claim: *Smith v Croft (No 2)* (1988)
   - where a more appropriate way of dealing with the matter was available: *Cooke v Cooke* (1997), where the claimant had also petitioned under s459 CA 1985; *Mumbray v Lapper* (2005), where either of the parties could have sought relief either by winding up on the just and equitable ground or under s459 (see section 11.3);
   - where the claim was made for personal reasons rather than for the benefit of the company: *Barrett v Duckett* (1995).

11.2.4 Companies Act 2006

1. In the course of the consultation process leading to the 2006 Act the Law Commission recorded a number of criticisms of the rule in *Foss v Harbottle* and the derivative claim: *Shareholder Remedies* (Law Com 246, 1997). It recommended partial abolition of the rule and a new derivative claim. This view was accepted by the Company Law Review. The *Final Report* recommended that derivative claims should be restricted to breaches of directors' duties and that they should be put on a statutory footing.

2. The long-established rule that directors owe duties to the company and not to individual shareholders is given statutory authority under s170 CA 2006.

3. Part 11 of the 2006 Act puts the derivative claim on a statutory footing and provides for a more flexible framework to allow a shareholder to pursue an action. Under the new provisions:
   - a shareholder will be able to bring a claim seeking relief on behalf of the company for a wrong done to the company, including for breach of duty on the part of directors of the company (s260);
   - the claimant will not be required to show wrongdoer control.

4. Section 261 provides for a two-stage procedure:
   - a *prima facie* case must be made to continue the action;
   - before the second stage the court may hear evidence provided by the company;
   - the court may then give permission for the derivative claim to be heard.

5. Section 263(3) sets out the factors that the court must take into account in considering whether to grant permission to continue the claim. These include:
   - whether the member is acting in good faith;
   - whether the company has decided not to pursue the action;
   - whether the act or omission in question gives rise to a claim that the member could pursue in his or her own right.

11.3 STATUTORY PROVISIONS: UNFAIR PREJUDICE

Section 459(1) CA 1985 provides that a member may petition the court 'on the ground that the company's affairs are being or have been conducted in a manner which is unfairly prejudicial to the interests of its members'. This section (first enacted as s75 CA 1980) replaced s210 CA 1948 which provided a remedy for 'oppressive' conduct and had been very restrictively interpreted by the courts.

11.3.1 Who can petition?

1. A claim may be made by:
   - members of the company;
   - those to whom shares have been transferred by operation of law, for example personal representatives, trustees in bankruptcy.
2. A member may only petition *as member*, but it is recognised that the interests of a member are not necessarily limited to consititutional rights. See for example *Re a company (No 00477 of 1986)*.
3. There is no requirement of 'clean hands' (in contrast to the remedy under s122(1)(g) Insolvency Act 1986) although the conduct of the petitioner may affect the remedy (*Re London School of Electronics* (1986)).

11.3.2 Meaning of 'unfairly prejudicial conduct'

1. Conduct must be both unfair and prejudicial (*Re BSB Holdings Ltd (No 2)* (1996)).
2. However, in contrast to the way the courts interpreted s210 of the 1948 Act, the terms 'unfair' and 'prejudicial' have been given a very wide interpretation.
3. The courts have employed the concept of the reasonable bystander in determining unfair prejudice.
4. There is no need, in proving unfairness, to show either intention or bad faith (*Re RA Noble & Sons (Clothing) Ltd*

(1983)). The test is whether it could be reasonably considered that the conduct unfairly prejudiced the petitioner's interests.

5. Prejudice does not necessarily require a reduction in the value of the petitioner's shareholding and may be shown in a number of ways:

   (a) exclusion from management (*Richards v Lundy* (2000));

   (b) failure to pay dividends (*Re Sam Weller & Sons Ltd* (1990));

   (c) payment of excessive remuneration to directors (*Re Cumana* (1986));

   (d) diversion of corporate assets or corporate opportunity (*Re London School of Electronics Ltd* (1986));

   (e) Packing the board with directors having interests adverse to the company (*Whyte, Petitioner* (1984)).

6. In general, mismanagement will not amount to unfair prejudice (*Re Elgindata Ltd* (1991)), but serious or gross mismanagement has been considered prejudicial (*Re Macro (Ipswich) Ltd* (1994)).

7. The section has been interpreted to include not only a breach of the company's constitution, but also a failure to meet the 'legitimate expectations' of a member or members. In the case of small private companies, the legitimate expectations may be outside of the constitution (*Re Saul D Harrison & Sons Ltd* (1994); *Richards v Lundy* (2000)). However, the courts have not been willing to recognise legitimate expectations beyond the constitution in the case of public companies (*Re Blue Arrow plc* (1987)). The law in this area has been discussed and clarified by the House of Lords in *O'Neill v Phillips* (1999). The concept of 'legitimate expectation' was applied restrictively in that case on the basis that there was no conclusive agreement between the parties on which it could be based.

11.3.3 The orders of the court

1. It is important to note the scope and flexibility of the orders.
   The court has freedom to make whatever order is deemed
   appropriate in the circumstances, but some specific orders are
   set out in s461. These are:
   - to regulate the company's affairs in future (*Re Harmer Ltd*
     (1958) – a case heard under the old s210);
   - to order the company to do or refrain from doing
     something;
   - to authorise civil proceedings;
   - to order the purchase of the petitioner's shares.
2. The most common remedy is an order of the court to
   purchase the shares of the petitioner. The following principles
   are applied:
   - the shares are normally purchased at their full value and are
     not discounted to reflect the fact that they represent a
     minority holding;
   - the conduct of the petitioner (for example if s/he was in
     any way to blame for the breakdown) may be relevant and
     the shares may be discounted to reflect this;
   - usually the valuation will be calculated as at the time of the
     order, but the court has discretion in fixing the date and
     may fix it at the time of the petition;
   - if the parties cannot agree, the price should be set by an
     independent valuer.

11.3.4 The future of the remedy?

1. Since its introduction, s459 has given minority shareholders
   an important remedy.
2. However, it has been criticised for the cost involved in
   bringing a case, for the length and complexity of cases and for
   the fact that it may allow minority shareholders to enforce
   their will over that of the majority.

3. In *O'Neill v Phillips* the House of Lords reviewed the development of the law relating to unfair prejudice and clarified many important aspects. The decision is likely to restrict the use of the section and its influence can be seen in recent cases, for example *Re GN Marshall Ltd* (2001)*; Re Phoenix Office Supplies Ltd* (2003).

11.3.5 Reform

1. The main concern of the Law Commission in its Report *Shareholder Remedies* (1997 CM 3769) Law Com No 246 was the length and complexity of the proceedings.

2. The Law Commission recommended that there should be a rebuttable presumption that where a shareholder has been excluded from participation in the management of the company the conduct will be presumed to be unfairly prejudicial by reason of the exclusion; and
  ● if the presumption is not rebutted and the court is satisfied that it ought to order a buy-out of the petitioner's shares, it should do so on a pro-rata basis (i.e. without any discount to reflect the fact that the petitioner's holding is a minority holding);
  ● winding up should be added to the remedies specified in s461;
  ● an 'exit provision' should be included in Table A.

3. However, the Company Law Steering Group in its *Final Report* did not accept these proposals. It recommended that 'in the interests of certainty and the containment of the scope of section 459 actions', the decision in *O'Neill v Phillips* should be accepted and the basis for a claim under section 459 should be breach of an agreement.

4. Under the 2006 Companies Act ss994–996 replace ss459–461.

11.4 WINDING UP ON THE JUST AND EQUITABLE GROUND

1. The Insolvency Act 1986 provides a rather drastic remedy for a dissatisfied shareholder, used mainly in situations involving small closely-held companies (sometimes called quasi-partnerships) where the relationship of trust and confidence has broken down.

2. Section 122(1)(g) provides that company may be wound up if the court is of the opinion that it is just and equitable that the company should be wound up.

3. Section 124 provides that an application can be made by anyone who is a contributory. A contributory is a person who is liable to contribute to the assets of a company in the event of its being wound up. A fully paid-up member who is not liable to contribute has to show that s/he has a tangible interest in the winding up.

11.4.1 Restrictions on the remedy

1. It is an equitable procedure, and there is therefore the requirement for 'clean hands'.

2. Section 125(2) provides that the court may not order a winding up if there is an alternative remedy available to the petitioners and they have been unreasonable in not accepting it (*Re a Company (No 002567 of 1982)* (1983)). However, there have been circumstances where the alternative remedy has not been appropriate and the application for winding up has succeeded (*Virdi v Abbey Leisure* (1990)).

11.4.2 Reasons for applications for just and equitable winding up

1. Successful petitions have been made on the following grounds:

- in the case of a quasi-partnership that the relationship of trust and confidence has broken down (*Re Yenidje Tobacco Co Ltd* (1916)). The breach must be sufficiently serious to justify the winding up;
- deadlock (*Ng Eng Hiam v Hg Kee Wei* (1964));
- lack of probity (*Loch v John Blackwood Ltd* (1924)). The fact that directors are negligent and inefficient is not sufficient to show lack of probity (*Five Minute Car Wash Service Ltd* (1966));
- loss of substratum of company (*Re German Date Coffee Co* (1882)).

2. In *Ebrahimi v Westbourne Galleries* (1973) Lord Wilberforce laid down general guidelines in cases involving quasi-partnerships and a breakdown of trust. There must have been:
- a breakdown of trust and confidence;
- reasonable expectation of taking part in the management of the company;
- a restriction on the sale of shares so that the petitioner is 'locked into' the company.

11.4.3 Scope of the remedy

1. In some cases where unfair prejudice cannot be shown, the court has ordered a winding up (*Re RA Noble (Clothing) Ltd* (1983)).
2. But a petition was refused in *Re Guidezone Ltd* (2000) on the ground that the proposition that winding up on the just and equitable ground is wider than s459 is inconsistent with *O'Neill v Phillips*.
3. The Law Commission has recommended that winding up should be added to the remedies available under s461 in order to streamline the procedures.

CHAPTER 12

TAKEOVERS AND MERGERS

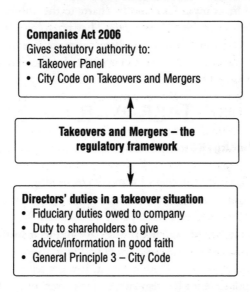

Companies Act 2006
Gives statutory authority to:
- Takeover Panel
- City Code on Takeovers and Mergers

Takeovers and Mergers – the regulatory framework

Directors' duties in a takeover situation
- Fiduciary duties owed to company
- Duty to shareholders to give advice/information in good faith
- General Principle 3 – City Code

Part 28 of the Companies Act 2006, which deals with takeovers, was brought into force on 6 April 2006. It gives statutory authority to the Takeover Panel and introduces a number of complex new provisions. This chapter focuses on the role of the Takeover Panel and the City Code on Takeovers and Mergers.

12.1 INTRODUCTION

1. A takeover is usually understood to mean the process by which one company gains control of another.
2. A merger is where the undertaking, property and liabilities of two or more companies are transferred to another company. This may be one of the original companies or it may be a new company. All or substantially all of the shareholders of the original companies become shareholders in the new company.

3. **Private companies** often have a provision in the articles of association allowing directors to refuse to register a transfer of shares, so that a takeover will not be possible without the authority and consent of the directors.

4. **Public companies** can offer shares to the public and may be listed on the Stock Exchange. They often have large and dispersed shareholdings. The usual procedure is for the offeror company to a send a circular to the shareholders in the offeree (or target) company making an offer to buy their shares.

12.2 THE TAKEOVER PANEL

12.2.1 Background

1. Following a number of scandals concerning takeovers and mergers, the Code on Takeovers and Mergers was published in 1967, and in 1968 a panel was established, made up of people with experience of the City and its institutions. Until May 2006 the Takeover Panel had no statutory authority and no legal powers of enforcement. It was a self-regulatory body, responsible for the regulation of takeovers of public companies in the UK within the framework of the self-regulatory rules contained in the City Code on Takeovers and Mergers.

2. In May 2006 the Takeover Directive (Interim Implementation) Regulations 2006, SI 2006/1183 came into force. This implemented the Takeover Directive (2004/25/EC) which set minimum standards on the regulation of takeovers of companies whose shares are traded on a regulated market.

3. Under the Directive member states are required to designate an authority to supervise takeover bids in accordance with rules made under the Directive. While the designated authority may be a non-statutory body, it must be recognised by national law. The regulations provided a statutory foundation for the work of the Takeover Panel.

4. The Takeover Directive required implementation by 20 May 2006 and the Takeover Directive (Interim Implementation) Regulations was a 'stopgap' measure to comply with EU law until the relevant sections of the Companies Act 2006 were brought into force. Part 28 of the Act, which implements the Directive, was brought into force on 6 April 2007 and the Regulations were repealed.

5. The 2006 Act provides a statutory foundation for the work of the Takeover Panel, signalling a shift away from self-regulation and providing a legislative framework.

12.2.2 Composition and functions of the Panel

1. The panel is composed of:
   - the Chairman and Deputy Chairman, appointed by the Bank of England;
   - members who are representatives of leading City institutions.

2. It has the following functions:
   (a) Legislative – it drafts the provisions of the Code and makes amendments.
   (b) Interpretive – it interprets the Code.
   (c) Monitoring/investigative – it establishes whether there has been a breach of the Code.
   (d) Enforcement – it ensures compliance with the Code:
   - If a breach is suspected, the company concerned is invited to appear before the Panel.
   - If it is shown that a breach has occurred the panel may issue either a private or a public reprimand, or the company may be reported to another United Kingdom or overseas authority or professional body, for example the Stock Exchange or the Financial Services Authority, which may take disciplinary action. The Panel can also publish a statement to the effect that the offender is someone who, in the opinion of the Hearing Committee, is not likely to comply with the code, which may result in members of

certain professional bodies being required not to act for that person in certain transactions.

- The consequences of non-compliance now also include criminal liability.

12.2.3 Judicial Review and the role of the court

1. It has been held that the Panel is subject to judicial review (*R v Panel on Takeovers and Mergers, ex parte Datafin* (1987); *R v Panel on Takeovers and Mergers, ex parte Guinness plc* (1990)).
2. The courts have recognised that the Panel is required to make decisions quickly and with authority and may give a ruling for future guidance rather than reverse a past decision.

12.3 THE CITY CODE ON TAKEOVERS AND MERGERS

1. Following implementation of the Takeover Directive and the 2006 Act, the rules set out in the code now have a statutory basis. The eighth edition of the Code was published on 20 May 2006 and was amended on 6 April 2007 to reflect its statutory status. It is a lengthy document, containing six General Principles and a number of detailed Rules.
2. The main objectives of the Code are:
   - to ensure fair and equal treatment of all shareholders in relation to takeovers;
   - to provide an orderly framework within which takeovers are conducted.
3. The Code is not concerned with:
   - the financial or commercial advantages or disadvantages of a takeover. These are matters for the company and its shareholders;
   - issues such as competition policy, which are the responsibility of government and are dealt with by separate legislation.

12.3.1 Principles underpinning the code

The general principles are statements of acceptable standards of commercial behaviour and reflect the principles set out in art 3 of the Directive. They are:

1. All holders of the securities of an offeree company of the same class must be afforded equivalent treatment; moreover if a person acquires control of a company, the other holders of securities must be protected.
2. The holders of securities of an offeree company must have sufficient time and information to enable them to reach a properly informed decision on the bid; where it advises the holders of securities, the board of the offeree company must give its views on the effects of implementation of the bid on employment, conditions of employment and the locations of the company's places of business.
3. The board of an offeree company must act in the interests of the company as a whole and must not deny the holders of securities the opportunity to decide on the merits of the bid.
4. False markets must not be created in the securities of the offeree company, of the offeror company or of any company concerned by the bid in such a way that the rise or fall of the prices of the securities becomes artificial and the normal functioning of the markets is distorted.
5. An offeror must announce a bid only after ensuring that he/she can fulfil in full any cash consideration, if such is offered, and after taking all reasonable measures to secure the implementation of any other type of consideration.
6. An offeree company must not be hindered in the conduct of its affairs for longer than is reasonable by a bid for its securities.

12.3.2 Enforcement

Until 20 May 2006, the Code did not have the force of law, but worked on the premise that 'those who seek to take advantage of the facilities of the securities markets in the United Kingdom should conduct themselves in matters relating to takeovers in accordance with best business standards and so according to the Code'. Section 955 CA 2006 now provides that the Panel may seek enforcement by the courts.

12.4 DIRECTORS' DUTIES IN A TAKEOVER

1. Directors owe fiduciary duties to the company (*Hogg v Cramphorn; Howard Smith Ltd v Ampol Petroleum Ltd* (1974)). This can give rise to conflicts of interest in a takeover situation, as in *Dawson International plc v Coats Patons plc* (1988). Directors also owe a duty to shareholders to ensure that any information and advice is given in good faith and is not misleading.
2. In addition, note General Principle 3 which requires directors of the offeree company to act in the interests of the company as a whole.

CHAPTER 13

COMPANY FAILURE
AND LIQUIDATION

The legal framework:
Insolvency Act 1986, as amended by:
• Insolvency Act 2000
• Enterprise Act 2002

Pre-insolvency procedures
• Company voluntary arrangements
• Scheme of arrangement s425 CA 1985
• Administration orders
• Receivers and administrative

COMPANY FAILURE AND LIQUIDATION

Winding up
Voluntary winding up:
• Members' voluntary winding up
• Creditors' voluntary winding up
Compulsory winding up

Creditor protection:
• Fraudulent trading
• Wrongful trading

13.1 THE LEGAL FRAMEWORK

1. The law governing insolvency and liquidation was changed and updated by the Insolvency Act 1985, following recommendations of the Cork Report, and is now contained in the Insolvency Act 1986. Further changes have been introduced by the Insolvency Act 2000 and the Enterprise Act 2002.
2. The changes were intended to introduce procedures to facilitate the survival of a company in financial difficulty.
3. It is necessary to distinguish between insolvency procedures and liquidation procedures. Not all insolvency procedures result in the liquidation of the company and in some circumstances (notably the members' voluntary winding up) a company that is not insolvent will be put into liquidation.

13.1.1 Objectives of corporate insolvency law

The following objectives have been suggested:

1. To facilitate the recovery of companies in financial difficulty.
2. To suspend the pursuit of rights and remedies of individual creditors.
3. To prevent transfers and transactions which unfairly prejudice the general creditors.
4. To divest directors of their powers of management in certain circumstances.
5. To ensure an orderly distribution of the estate and a fair system for the ranking of claims.
6. To impose responsibility for culpable management by directors and officers.

13.1.2 Insolvency practitioners

All liquidation and insolvency procedures require the appointment of an insolvency practitioner to a particular office as shown in the chart below.

Administrative receivership	Administrative receiver
Administration order	Administrator
Voluntary arrangement	Supervisor
Liquidation (voluntary or compulsory)	Liquidator

13.1.3 Qualification

(a) Only an individual can act as an insolvency practitioner, and he or she must not be:
  - an undischarged bankrupt;
  - subject to a director's disqualification order;
  - a patient within the meaning of the mental health legislation.
(b) He or she must be qualified to act generally: recognised professional bodies can authorise persons to act as insolvency practitioners.
(c) He or she must be qualified to act in relation to the particular company – s390.
(d) A person who acts without being qualified to do so commits a criminal offence.

13.2 PRE-INSOLVENCY PROCEDURES

13.2.1 Company voluntary arrangements

1. These are governed by the Insolvency Act 1986 as amended by the Insolvency Act 2000. In its original form, a company voluntary arrangement (CVA) did not provide for a moratorium on payment of the company's debts, which meant that it was possible that a creditor would petition for a winding up before the CVA could be agreed. The amended legislation provides for two kinds of CVA: without a

moratorium and with a moratorium.

2. Company voluntary arrangements without a moratorium:
   - a proposal is made for a composition in satisfaction of the company's debts or a scheme of arrangement;
   - a person who will supervise the implementation of the proposal, called the nominee, must be nominated;
   - the nominee must submit a report to the court indicating whether he or she thinks the proposal should be put to meetings of creditors and members;
   - if the nominee thinks the proposal should be put to meetings s/he must call separate meetings of all creditors (whose addresses are known) and members.

3. The proposal may be made by:
   - the directors of the company, where the company is not in administration or in liquidation;
   - the administrator if the company is in administration;
   - the liquidator where the company is being wound up.

4. A liquidator or administrator may act as nominee or may nominate another insolvency practitioner who will submit a report and then call meetings as above.

5. The meetings may approve or modify the proposal, but cannot approve an arrangement which deprives a secured creditor of his right to enforce the security without the consent of the creditor. Nor can they approve a proposal which alters the priority of preferential debts.

6. Once the proposal is approved, it binds all creditors who had notice and were entitled to vote at that meeting. However, there is a 28-day period within which application may be made to the court to have the proposal set aside.

7. Company voluntary arrangements with a moratorium are governed by the Insolvency Act 1986 Schedule A1. The procedure differs from a CVA without a moratorium in that:
   - the directors must apply for the moratorium;
   - they must give evidence that the company is likely to have sufficient funds to enable it to carry on business during the moratorium;

- they must submit to the nominee any information he requires to enable him to form an opinion;
- if the nominee forms a favourable opinion, the directors must file certain prescribed information with the court.

8. The effect of the moratorium is similar to an administration order, with the major difference that the directors retain their management role.

13.2.2 Scheme of arrangement under s425 Companies Act 1985

1. A compromise or arrangement may also be made under ss425–428 of the Companies Act, under which the rights of both creditors and members can be varied.
2. Under this procedure, a court order is required.
3. This will be governed by Part 26 CA 2006 when it comes into force (planned for April 2008).

13.2.3 Administration orders

1. The law relating to administration orders has been overhauled by the Enterprise Act 2002 and is now contained in Schedule B1 of the Insolvency Act 1986 as amended. Previously only the court could appoint an administrator. An administrator may now be appointed by:
   - the court – application may be made by the company or its directors or by a creditor;
   - out of court appointment by the company or its directors;
   - out of court appointment by the holder of a floating charge.
2. The legislation provides for an hierarchical list of purposes. The administrator must perform his or her role with the objective of:
   - rescuing the company as a going concern, or
   - achieving a better result for the company's creditors as a whole than would be achieved if the company were wound up before going into administration, or

- realising the property in order to make a distribution to one or more secured or preferential creditors.

3. The appointment of an administrator displaces the board of directors.

13.2.4 Receivers and administrative receivers: appointment

1. A receiver is an individual appointed to take control of property which is security for a debt.

2. Receivers may be appointed by the court or in accordance with the terms of a debenture. Normally there is a clause in the charge which entitles the chargee to appoint a receiver.

3. An administrative receiver may be appointed by a creditor whose debt is secured by a floating charge on the whole, or substantially the whole, of the company's undertaking. He or she takes control of the whole, or substantially the whole, of the company's property. There is overlap between the administrative receiver and the new administration regime.

13.2.5 Effect of appointment of administrative receiver

1. The administrative receiver has sole authority to deal with charged property.

2. The directors continue in office but have no authority to deal with the charged property, so their role is extremely limited.

3. An administrative receiver is an agent of the company until the company goes into liquidation (s44(1)(a)).

4. The administrative receiver must, within three months of appointment, prepare a report to be sent to the company's creditors and must call a meeting of unsecured creditors.

5. Apart from any contract for which specific performance may be ordered, the administrative receiver may cause the company to repudiate any existing contract.

13.3 WINDING UP

Winding up (liquidation) is the process whereby the company's assets are collected and realised, its debts paid and the net surplus distributed in accordance with the company's articles of association. Winding up is followed by dissolution of the company.

13.3.1 Voluntary winding up

The members adopt a resolution to wind up the company (special or extraordinary). This may result in a members' voluntary winding up or a creditors' voluntary winding up.

Members' voluntary winding up

1. The members of a company adopt a resolution to put the company into liquidation, following a statutory declaration by the directors that the company is able to pay its debts.
2. The members appoint a liquidator, usually at the meeting where the resolution to wind up the company is adopted.
3. On appointment of the liquidator, all powers of the directors cease.

Creditors' voluntary winding up

1. The members adopt a resolution to put the company into liquidation without a statutory declaration of solvency by the directors.
2. Members can nominate a liquidator, but the liquidator must hold a creditors' meeting at which they may nominate a liquidator, who will become the liquidator of the company unless the court directs otherwise.
3. The creditors may appoint a liquidation committee of up to five persons to act with the liquidator. Members may appoint five members to this committee.

13.3.2 Compulsory winding up

1. The court orders that the company be wound up on application to the court by a person entitled to petition. Section 124 provides that petitions may be made by:
   - any creditor who establishes a *prima facie* case;
   - contributories (shareholders who may contribute to the company's assets on liquidation);
   - the company itself;
   - the directors of the company;
   - a supervisor of a voluntary arrangement;
   - the clerk of the magistrates court if the company has failed to pay a fine;
   - any or all of the parties listed above together or separately;
   - the secretary of state;
   - an official receiver – if the company is already in voluntary liquidation;
   - an administrator of the company;
   - an administrative receiver of the company.
2. The vast majority of petitions are by creditors.
3. The grounds on which a petition may be made are contained in s122 Insolvency Act 1986. The most important are:
   - the company is unable to pay its debts (s122(1)(a));
   - it is just and equitable to wind it up (s122 (1)(g).

13.3.3 Appointment of liquidator

1. The official liquidator attached to the court where the order is made will be appointed.
2. If there are substantial assets, an insolvency practitioner may be appointed to replace the official liquidator.
3. Once the liquidator is appointed the directors cease to have any right to manage the company.
4. The role of the liquidator is to realise the assets and distribute them to those entitled to payment.
5. In an insolvent liquidation priority of payment is important:

    (a) where a debt is secured the asset charged may be taken in settlement of the debt;

    (b) the principle of set-off will allow a creditor who is owed money by the company to deduct the difference before paying the company, thus in effect receiving full payment of his debt to the company.

6. Subject to these two principles, the order of payment is;

- expenses of the winding up
- preferential debts
- general creditors
- deferred debts, for example debts due to a shareholder in his capacity as such, like dividends declared but not paid
- shareholders.

13.4 FRAUDULENT AND WRONGFUL TRADING

13.4.1 Fraudulent trading

1. Where a person (often, but not only, a director of a company) was involved in running a company which was operated with the intention of defrauding creditors, the liquidator can apply to the court for an order that the person must contribute towards the assets of the company (s213 Insolvency Act 1986).

2. In addition to civil liability, the director may be disqualified under the Company Directors Disqualification Act 1986 or prosecuted under s458 CA 1985.

3. To establish fraud, intention or recklessness must be proved (*R v Grantham* (1984)).

13.4.2 Wrongful trading

1. A liquidator may apply for an order that a director (defined as in s213) is liable to contribute to the company's assets if it can be shown that:

- the company has gone into insolvent liquidation;
- at some time before the start of the winding up, the director knew or ought to have known that there was no prospect of the company not going into insolvent liquidation; and
- the director was a director at the time of the relevant transaction (s214 Insolvency Act 1986).

2. The director's conduct should be judged against the standard of a reasonably diligent person having both:
   - the knowledge, skill and experience that would reasonably be expected of someone carrying out the same function; and
   - the knowledge, skill and experience of the director himself.

3. One of the problems with these provisions is that if the compensation is paid, it usually benefits the holders of a floating charge, rather than the unsecured creditors, whereas the legislation was initially designed to help unsecured creditors.

INDEX